COME TALK WITH ME

DEVELOPING THE SKILL
OF COMMUNICATING WITH GOD

BUDDY WESTBROOK

WITH CONNIE WILLEMS

Come Talk with Me: Developing the Skill of Communicating with God
by C.L. (Buddy) Westbrook

Printed in the United States of America
First edition 2011

ISBN 9781613790816

For permission please contact author at: www.ComeTalkwithMe.com

Some of the personal accounts and dialogues shared in this book are true to life and are used by permission of the person or persons. Other illustrations are composites.

www.xulonpress.com

To the Lord God, for this is His.
He is the One who taught me how to communicate with Him,
and He is the One who gave the words I have taught over and over
as well as the words to write this book.

❖

And to my precious wife, Letty.
This book represents my life work, and Letty has been greatly
used by the Lord to help forge this message into my life.
She is my soul mate and has owned for herself all that is in this book
as well as skillfully supported, assisted, encouraged,
and put up with me.

CONTENTS

ACKNOWLEDGMENTS

So many have participated with me in this "life work" undertaking. I thank all of you for so vulnerably sharing yourself and your emerging relationships with God as I have coached you. You all have been my joy and have allowed me to watch our Father and learn so much more from Him. I thank you.

I thank the members of my church, who have actively supported and encouraged me throughout this entire process and have given me time to accomplish such a task; and thanks to Ron Carter for making it happen.

I thank Kimberlee Love, who was God's burr in my saddle and simply would not allow me to ignore God's call to write this book. Thanks for believing in me.

I thank Cynthia Bezek, who made me see that writing this book must happen and that it was truly possible. Thanks, Cynthia, for believing in me and giving so much.

I thank my book partner and editor, Connie Willems, who has listened to the Lord along with me, invested so much of herself and her time, and has helped enable this book to become all that God wanted.

I thank my friends and donors for their tangible investment in God's project and for all the skillful intercession.

I thank my wife, daughter, son-in-law, and granddaughter for the hundreds of hours you have walked with me in this project, actively helped me, loved me, and supported me.

Introduction

If I could give my readers one beginning exhortation, it would be this: "Do not read this book." That's right. I said, "Do not read this book." But before you close it and put it away, let me explain.

This is a book you *do*, not a book you simply read.

My years of ministry have been characterized by a coaching style of leadership. I love working with people in a hands-on fashion, and my greatest joy is to help them discover and experience personal, intimate relationship with our perfect Father—relationship that is experienced by talking *with* Him. I have seen many learn how to talk with God freely and hear what He has to say to them personally and individually through a satisfying exchange as described by the Lord Jesus in the Scriptures.

Yet this is not what most Christians experience. As a result, they are left somewhat dissatisfied about prayer. They don't like to admit it, but they are sometimes bored, often stuck, sometimes feeling stagnant. Something doesn't seem to be *working*, not only with prayer but also with their relationships with God, yet they can't put their finger on what is wrong.

More than a decade ago, some prominent Christian leaders convened for the purpose of addressing the serious problem of church decline. They sensed apathy, especially among the youth, and their plan was to create materials that would assess a person's spiritual growth, identify areas of deficiency, and then provide appropriate resources. A friend who was a leader in this movement told me about the project. As I listened to him, I began thinking about what it seemed they were trying to discover: What *really* causes transformation in Christians' lives?

Curious, I embarked on a pursuit of the answer. I considered some excellent discipleship programs; looked at key leaders with lots of followers; thought about the already abundant supply of superb study materials. Here is what I concluded. All of these programs and materials were excellent; yet the church was still in such a condition that these prominent Christian leaders were compelled to try to figure out how to reverse this trend.

I was confused. So I asked the Lord, "Father, would You help me understand? I know You want all of Your kids to look more and more like our Lord Jesus Christ. I know You want followers of Jesus Christ, not just church attendees or people who silently believe in You. I know that none of these resources seem to have any true guarantee. I am not necessarily looking for something with a guarantee, but I would like to know what You would say causes Christians to grow."

Here is what I believe He said to me. *"My son, this is a great pursuit. You are absolutely correct; I do want every one of My sons and daughters to grow, to mature, to look more and more like Mine. And yes, these programs are excellent. But there will never be a program that will guarantee growth.*

"Here is, as you say it, what causes transformation: It is coming into My presence. Anyone who comes into My presence cannot remain the same. Either they will be greatly softened or they will be hardened. Most will have their hearts softened. All who continue to relationally and experientially come into My presence will grow; they will change and mature. The more time they spend relationally with Me, the more they will become like Me."

I cannot tell you how exciting this thought was. It has changed and formed my life. I am committed to showing Christians how to practically "enter into God's presence" through relational, two-way prayer. I am committed to teach many how to talk *with* God, not just talk *to* Him.

I have had the privilege of leading individuals, Bible-study groups, and congregations through coaching in this very thing: learning the transforming ways of intimate communication with Almighty God. My approach to this ministry reminds me of my training as an athlete. There, I learned that to excel I needed far more than information about the fundamentals; I needed to try out basic skills and then build on them under the guidance of a personal, hands-on coach. In a similar way, relational prayer is something we can build and develop as God leads us. I did not think that the coaching ministry God has developed within me could be effectively applied to a book. However, as I put this course into writing, God did remarkable things and provided in remarkable ways.

One of those divine provisions, and a key aspect of developing this project, has been the involvement of Connie Willems. I first knew Connie, who was then managing editor of *Discipleship Journal* (published by The Navigators), as a student in one of my courses on communicating with God. Through dialoging with God, she became transformed in her experience of prayer and intimate relationship with the Lord. God then put within her a desire to help train others in this ministry. Now she has collaborated with me on this book. Part of her unique contribution is through shaping the assignments and training instructions that will enable you to practice, evaluate, and build your ability to talk and relate with God.

The training tools in this book are modeled after the ones I use in face-to-face ministry coaching. Each chapter concludes with a "Practice Session," where you'll find an assignment carefully designed to enable you to try out the skills taught in the chapter. You'll receive examples, coaching, and help to address common problems and misconceptions.

To best receive what God has for you it is important that you actively participate, whether you're working through this book on your own or with a group. You'll want to first read through the chapter and complete the original assignment; then take an additional time during the week to work through the follow-up coaching for that assignment. Obviously God will be your personal coach, but I trust He will use the explanations and assignments to facilitate the communication He deeply desires for every one of His own.

Consider the words of the great hymn, "In the Garden," by C. Austin Miles:

> And He walks with me, and He talks with me,
> And He tells me I am His own.
> And the joy we share as we tarry there,
> None other has ever known.

Do these words describe what prayer is like for you? Do you experience God talking with you and transforming you regularly, daily? Do you hear Him telling you in a personal and individual way that you are His own? Do you have confidence whenever you talk with Him that you will hear His voice? Do you feel as if you share a joy with Him that is rare? If not, you can. He's waiting for you.

> My heart has heard you say, "Come and talk with me." And my heart responds, "LORD, I am coming."   (Psalm 27:8, NLT)

COMMUNICATING WITH GOD

Many years ago I was reading Matthew 10, where Jesus explained to His disciples the plan for His Kingdom. I had read this passage many times, but this day one verse unsettled me:

> He who loves father or mother more than Me is not worthy of Me; and he who loves son or daughter more than Me is not worthy of Me. (verse 37, NASB)

Here was my problem: I loved Jesus, but I *adored* my wife and daughter.

I had never admitted to myself, much less anyone else, that I loved Letty and Windy more than I loved Jesus. I guess I didn't think it really mattered as long as I truly loved all three of them.

But I believe the Bible is God's accurate and infallible Word. As I kept reading this verse, I could not figure out any possible meaning for it other than what Jesus said. Apparently, because I did not love Him more than my wife or my daughter, I was "not worthy" of Him.

I felt I was being penalized for how much I loved my family! So I began pursuing the Lord over this. I wanted to know why He chose to make such an impossible comparison the standard for being worthy of Him. It did not take long before God helped me understand the problem.

THE "IMPOSSIBLE" RELATIONSHIP

In addition to being a pastor, I am a licensed professional counselor and am supposed to be somewhat of a "communication" expert. I know that true closeness in a relationship is based upon communication. With my wife, Letty, I feel loved and cared for, important and valued, mainly through our conversations and the many things Letty tells me. She and I have worked diligently to learn how to communicate with each other; without good communication, we simply could not have the exceptional relationship we enjoy today.

But I had to admit this same relational connection didn't exist between God and me. Sure, I communicated with Him. I spoke to Him in prayer. I brought my needs and concerns to Him, praised and worshiped Him, confessed my sins, and shared my problems. I read and studied—even taught—His Word, the Bible. But all this was just not the same as what I enjoyed with Letty.

I realized the difference: I talked *to* God, but I talked *with* Letty. When Letty and I talked, we both shared with each other; we both listened to and received from each other. Yet with the Lord God Almighty, I did the talking. There were times I felt He communicated to me, but these were sporadic and mostly occurred through words from the Bible (or sometimes through other people or nature).

Then I wondered about Christians who hardly knew the Bible; how could God communicate with them? Surely I would never say to a new Christian, "Go ahead and pray and make sure you read and study the Bible. Then after a few years, when you know the Bible much better,

God may—from time to time—communicate with you through His written Word. But remember to love Him more than you love your parents and spouse and kids."

It was then I realized there must be more to a relationship with God than I had known. If I wanted to experience great closeness and intimacy with Him and love Him more than my wife or daughter, as Jesus commanded me, I must learn how to communicate *with* Him and not just *to* Him.

That meant rethinking prayer.

Prayer? Really?

Most Christians feel shame and guilt over the amount of time we devote to prayer. Most of us know prayer is extremely important and feel we should pray more, yet we have a difficult time disciplining ourselves to do it. In my early years as a Christian, I looked at prayer very much as I do most things: practically and pragmatically. I didn't particularly like or dislike prayer. It was a good thing to do, so I did it. I praised God because I should, and I talked to Him about things I needed. But I didn't waste any words—in fact, I think I tended to use as few words as possible. My prayers weren't relational at all. They were more of an official transaction. I didn't think about prayer much, but if I did, I figured it couldn't hurt and might help, though I didn't expect much. If God chose to do something I asked for, that was a plus.

As I was searching for how to relate with God in prayer, I began to consider what I had learned in my counseling classes about communication. There, I learned that a healthy relationship includes loving, enjoying, sharing, trusting, spending time together, giving and receiving, caring for each other, and so on. Communication is at the center of each of these. In order to feel loved or cared for or enjoyed, we must communicate with one another. To trust, we must communicate vulnerably at a deep level. These classes had caused me to

3

change how I talked and interacted with Letty, and our relationship grew and deepened as a result.

So I had to stop and consider: If God wants me to have that kind of relationship with my wife, and if He can lead me into that with her, then maybe a relational God who teaches this kind of relational stuff could show me how to do that with Him as well.

And He has. I can't tell you the exact process He used with me because it happened gradually, over decades, as I explored and prodded. And frankly, I wasn't taking notes. But I was beginning to experience Him more tangibly and literally; I was beginning to communicate *with* Him. I was praying, but it was far different from what I'd been used to. I was learning to share myself deeply with God and expect Him to reply and talk to me about His thoughts and His feelings. This new way of communicating created a new relationship between us.

Even though I'm a man, and we men are schooled to think we don't really need or want intimacy, I was discovering that underneath it all, I *did* want intimacy. God's command for me to love Him more than anyone else was leading me into exactly what I wanted, even though I had been reluctant to acknowledge it.

My experience of prayer is now totally different. Prayer is relational, experiential—even shocking. Shocking in the sense that I can go to God in a foul mood, *knowing* there is nothing that could make me feel better, and I come out helped and *changed*. I receive something every time I go to God in prayer. I *experience* something. Most times I'm surprised by something He says—sometimes pleasantly so, sometimes not so pleasantly. Without question, my relationship with God is now the deepest, most satisfying relationship I have, because I am talking *with* Him.

Talking with God

For many years now I have had the privilege of teaching others about this kind of prayer in a course I simply call "Communicating with

God." I've learned most Christians are where I was: Their prayers are a monologue. They talk to—or *at*—God, not *with* Him.

Let me share a typical conversation I have with someone in my course. I'll call him "James."

"Did you talk with your wife this morning?" I'll ask.

"Yes, of course," James will say.

"What did you talk about?"

"Well, for one thing, what we were going to do tonight."

"What did you say ... and what did she say?" James' wife might not believe it, but James tells me what both of them said.

Then I ask, "Did you have the opportunity to have a quiet time or pray this morning?"

"Yes, I did."

"I'm curious. Would you say the time of prayer was a monologue or dialogue?"

James pauses for a moment and then says, "I think I would say it was dialogue."

"What did you talk about?"

James shares that he talked to God about a difficult issue at work and about concerns for one of his children.

"What did God say?" I ask.

James looks blank. "What do you mean?" he asks.

"Well you could tell me about the dialogue you had with your wife this morning—what you said and what she said. You said your prayer time with the Lord was also a dialogue, so when you said these things to God, what did He say in response?"

From there the conversation becomes surprisingly predictable. When I ask that question, many people simply look blank. Others answer like James does, after a long pause. "Oh, well, I was reading in Luke ... "

"Wait, I just want to know what God *said*, not what you read."

James thinks for a bit and then shrugs, "Well, I guess it really was more of a monologue than a dialogue."

These types of replies trouble me. This is not what our Heavenly Father wants from us in prayer. He is not into gathering information from us about our lives. And He doesn't want us to pray just because He said to do it. His desire is not our obedience from a sense of duty or obligation; He will accept this kind of prayer but it is not His heart. You see, what God wants is *us*. He wants a relationship with us, He wants us to know Him, experience Him, and enjoy our relationship with Him. God is all about relationship, not about servants who are faithful and who just transfer information to Him. So when we pray, our Father desires communication *with* us, not just communication *from* us.

This book is going to show you how to enter into two-way communication with God so you can receive His attention, care, affection, and loving words as an everyday part of your life.

How do we start? By considering how Jesus taught His followers to engage with His Father.

Practice Session

I want you to learn how to communicate *with* our Heavenly Father. Therefore, at the end of each chapter, it will be your turn to practice what we've talked about. This relationship with God isn't something that simply happens, it's something you do. So you'll get the most out of this course if you dig in and *do* the practices with me.

For this chapter, answer the questions below (I'll start giving you exercises to practice after the next chapter.) You may want to use a dedicated "class" notebook or journal for this. Or, if you're like many people and prefer to type your answers, you can visit www.ComeTalkwithMe.com to download a "course notebook" that you can use for all your practice sessions.

1. How would you answer the question I asked James, "Would you say your prayers are more of a monologue or a dialogue?"

2. What are your thoughts about learning to communicate *with* God? Do you have any doubts? Reservations? Hopes? Write a brief letter to God, telling Him what you think. Here is an example of how you might start: *"Dear God, I'm starting this course on communicating with You, and I'm not sure what I think about it ... "*

THE LORD'S LESSON ON PRAYER

O ver the years, I have asked many people a simple question in my course on communicating with God: "When Jesus' disciples asked Him, 'Lord, teach us to pray,' what did He teach them?"

Many people correctly identify part of His lesson plan. "The Lord's Prayer," they answer.

But I have never yet had someone give the complete answer. Never.

If so few Christians know the actual content of the one time God gave His specific lesson on how to pray, then what is the chance we are following His instructions accurately and skillfully? Probably not much.

We generally recite the Lord's Prayer from Matthew 6. I suspect this is why so many Christians do not know Jesus' complete lesson on prayer. To find the whole story, we must also go to Luke 11. If we look at Jesus' lesson there, here is what it would look like in outline form:

The Content of Prayer (verses 2-4). Jesus first gives us what we call the Lord's Prayer, which provides the topics for our prayers.

The Manner of Prayer (verses 5-12). Then, through two word pictures—of a best friend with a best friend and of a child with a loving parent—Jesus gives the manner in which we should pray.

The Provision for Prayer (verse 13). Finally, Jesus teaches that if we communicate with God as our best friend and our perfect, loving parent, not only will God respond, He will give us Himself: God the Holy Spirit.

Let's look at the three parts of this lesson plan in more depth. My experience is that when we follow Jesus' teaching and learn how to communicate *with* God instead of *to* Him, prayer becomes our most important life skill and something we actually look forward to and enjoy.

THE CONTENT OF PRAYER: THE LORD'S PRAYER

Jesus started His lesson by saying, "When you pray, say: 'Father, hallowed be your name, your kingdom come. Give us each day our daily bread. Forgive us our sins, for we also forgive everyone who sins against us. And lead us not into temptation'" (Luke 11:2-4).

For many years I saw the Lord's Prayer simply as a model prayer. The only time I thought about or recited it was at funerals, at churches, or at some community activity where someone thought it would be good to pray. I did not see any ongoing personal application for it.

Then a few years ago I was struck with verse 3: "Give us each day our daily bread." *Just how often should I pray for* daily *bread?* I wondered. Suffice it to say, the Lord showed me that "daily" meant just that. That compelled me to ask Him about the rest of the prayer. Was all of this model prayer to be prayed daily or just the "bread" part? I am convinced He said the whole prayer is to be used daily.

Praying this prayer daily opened up a whole new line of communication with my Father. Over the years, as He and I have used this prayer as a basis for many conversations, I have seen again and again that at the start of each day I don't have what I need to have and I don't know what I need to know. I don't have my daily provision; I don't know what His will is for my day; I don't know what sins to confess or what temptation is in my path. But God does. And if I will just come and ask Him, He is delighted to share with me.

He reinforced this to me from Isaiah 55:1-3 (emphasis added):

> Come, all you who are thirsty, come to the waters; and you who have no money, come, buy and eat! Come, buy wine and milk without money and without cost. Why spend money on what is not bread, and your labor on what does not satisfy? *Listen, listen to me,* and eat what is good, and your soul will delight in the richest of fare. *Give ear and come to me: hear me,* that your soul may live. I will make an everlasting covenant with you, my faithful love promised to David.

If I choose simply to *come* and *listen* to Him, I will have all I need. But even more, I clearly see that life with our Father isn't about just functioning. I have now learned that if I come and listen, my Heavenly Father gives me the "richest of fare"—the abundant life Jesus promises in John 10:10.

Now I pray the Lord's model prayer each day and I've found it to be an incredibly rich, daily feast that gives me all I need. In the next chapter I'll walk through it phrase by phrase with you and show you the incredible relationship and provision it brings. But before we do that, we need to consider the rest of the lesson Jesus taught about prayer so that we approach prayer in the manner Jesus wants us to.

THE MANNER OF PRAYER:
RELATING WITH OUR FRIEND AND FATHER

I picture that when the disciples asked Jesus to teach them how to pray, Jesus thought it a very important question—but without a simple answer. Prayer involves real beings (us) communicating with a real being (God) in a real relationship. When humans communicate, we use our physical senses. I see my friends with my eyes, hear them with my ears, touch them with a hug or a handshake. But I have never seen or heard or touched God. Personally, I am not expecting to until I join Him in heaven!

I picture Jesus thinking about the problem of teaching humans how to communicate with a Person, whom we cannot see with our eyes or hear with our ears or touch with our hands. He wanted to draw upon common denominators we all experience in our important relationships, so He chose to illustrate prayer by using the relationship of a friend with a friend and a child with a father. His other teachings are full of pictures of masters and servants, employers and stewards, landowners and tenants. Yet here Jesus follows up His model prayer with an explanation involving two very personal relationships:

> Then [Jesus] said to them, "Suppose one of you has a friend, and he goes to him at midnight and says, 'Friend, lend me three loaves of bread, because a friend of mine on a journey has come to me, and I have nothing to set before him.'
>
> "Then the one inside answers, 'Don't bother me. The door is already locked, and my children are with me in bed. I can't get up and give you anything.'
>
> "I tell you, though he will not get up and give him the bread because he is his friend, yet because of the man's boldness he will get up and give him as much as he needs.
>
> "So I say to you: Ask and it will be given to you; seek and you will find; knock and the door will be opened to you. For everyone who asks receives; he who seeks finds; and to him who knocks, the door will be opened.

"Which of you fathers, if your son asks for a fish, will give him a snake instead? Or if he asks for an egg, will give him a scorpion?

"If you then, though you are evil, know how to give good gifts to your children, how much more will your Father in heaven give the Holy Spirit to those who ask him!"   (Luke 11:5-13)

For many years I wondered about the friend picture in this passage, where the man goes to his friend's house looking for bread. It seems to demonstrate "annoying persistence" more than anything else. Is persistence in prayer really the point here, as we often teach? If that's the case, why didn't Jesus just talk about persistence, as He did with the widow and the judge in Luke 18; why mix in the idea of friendship?

It's Jesus' commentary on the second picture, that of a child with a father, that gives us our clue. There, He says, "If you then, *though you are evil*, know how to give good gifts ... " (verse 13). Both word pictures are based on core relationships common to all of us: "friend" and "parent." Every friendship and child-parent relationship—even the very best ones—are flawed, because, like Jesus says, we are "evil." Yet there are still very great benefits in these two special relationships.

In the friend picture, Jesus is actually describing a *very* good friendship. Even though friendship can often "knock" at inopportune times, and even though people may not have the best of hearts or even the best motives, a good friend—even when he's annoyed and irritated—can still be counted on.

Jesus makes the same point in the child-parent picture. Even though good fathers have a sinful nature and maybe their words and manners aren't always the best, they can still be counted on. Parents may be in an awful mood or really upset with their kids, yet there is no chance they're going to slip their kids a snake or a scorpion instead of giving them a peanut butter and jelly sandwich.

The most basic assumption we make of friends or parents is that they will come through for us. Granted, that doesn't always happen; we've all had awful friends and some of us have had unhealthy, even damaging, parents. But most of us can expect some extent of "being there for us" from these two relationships.

Watch what Jesus then does in both of these pictures. He follows the supposition with a comparison to what God is like as our Good Friend and Good Father.

Immediately after the friend picture, Jesus shows what happens when we pray: "Everyone who asks receives; he who seeks finds; and to him who knocks, the door will be opened" (verse 10). When we ask God for something, He gives it, and when we seek in prayer, we find, and when we knock on *God's* door, He opens it for us. When we go to our Heavenly Friend, we are knocking on the actual door to the throne room of God, and it opens to us, and we find what we are looking for. This is *infinitely* superior to having a friend we can count on at midnight! God is the Friend who is faithful, trustworthy, wise, forgiving, honest, loving, selfless, generous, kind, humble, gentle, patient, strong, protective, and understanding.

The comparison of God as our Good Father leads us to the third part of His lesson on prayer: the provision that makes this manner of communication possible.

THE PROVISION FOR PRAYER: THE GIFT OF GOD HIMSELF

Verse 13 shows us the ultimate expression of God's fatherhood: "If you then, though you are evil, know how to give good gifts to your children, how much more will your Father in heaven give the Holy Spirit to those who ask Him!" When we come to our Perfect Father seeking what we need, He responds by giving us the Holy Spirit. This gift means God actually gives us Himself!

But didn't we all receive the Holy Spirit when we accepted Jesus Christ as our Lord and Savior? If so, what is God saying He will give us? I think it is kind of like what happens when a child loses connection with a parent. It's common for many children to distance themselves from their parents for a time when they are growing up, perhaps because of a striving after independence, or because of rebelliousness, or maybe because their parents are nerds—or for whatever reason. When children pull away, they are still part of the family but they are receiving little everyday benefit from having good parents. Practically speaking, they lose access to their parents' wisdom, protection, comfort, encouragement, and support. But when they reconnect and "ask" for parenting, what happens? They again receive the full benefits of their mother and father's parenting.

I believe it is the same here. God the Holy Spirit lives within us and is always with us. But rarely does He impose His presence and His will. And many of us rarely ask for Him. Many of us spend most of our lives somewhat separated from the incredible benefits of God's parenting.

Just like when teens humble themselves and return, asking for their parents' love and input and involvement, when we ask the Holy Spirit to come and rule and direct and protect and comfort (and on and on), we receive the full benefits from being children of a Parent who loves us and is committed to us. We receive God plus all the benefits inherent in Him.

This, I believe, is the ultimate outcome of learning how to communicate with the almighty, majestic God of the universe—we get to experience God personally and relationally!

EXPERIENCING JESUS' LESSON ON PRAYER

If we actually receive God Himself, this changes everything. Most people who haven't experienced genuine friendship and healthy, good parenting are stunted relationally. Unless they experience significant healing, they have virtually no chance of establishing healthy, vibrant relationships. They live (perhaps without a conscious awareness of it) on a constant quest to be loved and cared for. If deficits in human relationships genuinely cripple people, what happens to us when we do not experience our Creator as our Friend and Father? We miss out on the best friendship we will ever experience and we miss out on the foundational blessing of our Father's perfect parenting. This leaves significant wounds and holes in our lives.

This is why this unparalleled lesson on prayer by God Himself is compelling. If we truly understand and experience God as better than our best friend and the greatest parent we could ever fathom, try to imagine what such abundance of life would look like; try to imagine how rich would be this "richest of fare!"

As our Friend and as our Father, the Lord God wants to lavish us with all that He is and love on us in ways that are beyond our ability to comprehend. Not only is He good, He is *perfect!* As we have seen in Luke 11, even finite and flawed human relationships have genuine benefits that we can count on. How much more a perfect and flawless Friend and Father! All of us want someone we can always count on, who will always be with us and for us; this is who our God is.

Our part is that we must approach God with the boldness we would use with a best friend or deeply trusted parent, pouring out our hearts, sharing our struggles, and celebrating our victories—asking Him lots and lots of questions, asking for help, asking for whatever— and then *know* we can count on this perfect Friend and Father to answer us. If necessary, we are to keep on seeking and knocking, but making certain we expect an answer. We are to listen very carefully for anything He may say to us, not just what we want to hear. In the next chapter, I will show you how I do this with the Lord's model prayer that He taught to His disciples.

As I share these truths with Christians, they are excited and encouraged and hopeful. They begin to believe what they have often sensed: There is much more available to them. The problem never has been that Christians do not want to pray or that they are too busy. The problem is they do not know how to pray; they don't know the incredible gifts that are waiting for them when they follow Jesus' instructions. Once they know what to do and then follow those instructions, so much begins to change.

Practice Session

Skills You're Acquiring and Practicing

- Talking with God as your Perfect Father and Friend
- Learning to expect that God wants to respond to you

A Note to Men: I am a man and I know our gender does not like to read books with assignments, much less actually do the assignments. I certainly don't. However, before you dismiss the idea, I implore you just to look it over. Look at the samples and the coaching. Then think through this question: "Do I know how to do this?" If you don't, please ask the Lord if this is something He wants for you at this time. If you sense it is not, that's okay. If you sense this is His will for you at this time, please try the first couple of assignments.

My deepest desire for this book is to assist believers to learn how to communicate *with* our Heavenly Father by following the instructions in Luke 11. I want you to acquire skills, not just knowledge. I believe that relating with God is a skill like any other, one that we can develop. Therefore, in each practice session, you'll find

- The skills we'll focus on
- Your assignment
- Some pointers to keep in mind
- Follow-up coaching to sharpen your skills

Your Assignment

In this practice session, you will write a letter to God and then speculate on how He would reply back to you. You may do this in your own notebook or visit www.ComeTalkwithMe.com to download a free "course notebook" file in which you can type all your exercises in these practice sessions.

Step One: Your Letter to God

Write a letter to God expressing yourself as you would if you were talking with a best friend or with a perfect and loving parent. I suggest you start with "Dear God," and close with a salutation such as "Love," "Your friend," or whatever you choose.

Step Two: "God's" Letter to You

Write a letter from God back to you, speculating on what you think the Lord would say in response to what you have written. Anticipate He will sound like a best friend or outstanding parent. Again, start out with "Dear Joe," and close with "Love, God," "Sincerely, God," or whatever feels best for now.

Some people are uncomfortable writing such a letter. They think it is sacrilegious or inappropriate to try to speak for God. However, I am not asking you to speak *for* God but simply to speculate about what He might say, based on what you know of His character as revealed in the Bible, and the manner of prayer Jesus has given us.

Maybe this will make it easier. Let's say you're discussing an issue with one of your friends, and your friend asks, "What do you think your spouse (or good friend) would say about this?" Because you know your spouse, you'd probably have a good idea of what he or she would say. In a similar way, use what you know of God through the Bible to write a possible letter from God back to you.

Pointers

- *Relationship pictures.* Talk to God as you would talk to a good friend or a *very* good parent. Use natural language, not "prayer words" or phrases.

- *Personal.* The best content for your letter is something personal about you or about your relationship with God. For now, no prayer for other people.

- *Simple.* It's easier to speculate on God's response if you stick to one topic.

- *Avoid great pain.* For now, avoid talking about an area of great pain or difficulty, such as the death of a loved one or a lifelong struggle or a past great wrong or something about God that confuses you. Opening up areas of pain or struggle often makes the letter writing too difficult at this early stage.

- *Don't get hung up on the writing aspect.* You don't need to be "a writer," and I am not asking you to keep a journal. Putting these letters into writing is simply a tool to help you develop new skills. Also, this will give you a baseline that we can refer to later.

Sample: Here is a sample of the kind of letters you might write.

Dear God,

This is awkward. I do want to learn how to communicate with you better so I guess I will try to do this.

Today I am concerned about this project that I am working on. I don't feel I have all the information I need and that makes me feel insecure. My boss is putting pressure on me to get it done, but I know this isn't personal. Still, I am having trouble sleeping, and I know all this is making me irritable.

Until Bill finishes his part I'm just not sure what to do. I want to do my best and right now I'm not sure what that would be. Please help me deal with all this and help me be less irritable. Thanks for listening.

Love, John

Dear John,

Thanks for writing to me. I know you aren't crazy about this, but it means a lot to Me that this is important enough to you to try this.

I do know that this project is getting to you. Times like this are hard. I like talking to you about stuff like this because I am a Father who wants His children to come to Me and ask for what they need.

Right now you don't have all you need and there is little you can do until Bill finishes his part. It is good you see that. It is also good you are so responsible that delays like this bother you.

How about you pray for Bill, and I will help him with his part. Also, please tell your spouse about how much this is bothering you so she can pray for you and be sensitive to your stress.

Tonight when you get ready for bed, ask Me to help you sleep, then listen to that music that calms you down for about ten minutes. I will help you sleep better tonight.

Love, God

Follow-up Coaching

As I've helped many people learn to dialogue with God, I've found that coaching is essential. After you've completed each assignment, I will ask you a series of questions that prompt you to consider what went well and help you deal with problems or blocks. At times I will give you follow-up exercises and suggestions.

If you have not yet written your letters, please take the time to do so before you work through the following coaching.

1. Key indicators. To start with, lets consider a benchmark for your letters. Your letters went well if

❖ You wrote them, even if they felt uncomfortable or awkward.
❖ You kept to one topic or incident—something ordinary, not a place of great pain or struggle.
❖ You said what you thought and felt about the topic or incident.
❖ You talked to God as you would talk with a best friend or very good parent.
❖ Your speculation letter from God replied specifically rather than in broad generalities.
❖ The speculation letter from God was written as if a Good Friend or a Perfect Father were talking.

How did you do on these indicators? Write your thoughts in your notebook.

2. Blocked by a misconception about God. If you didn't feel your letters went well, don't worry. You will have more time to practice. However, you may also have experienced a key block, which I wish to address early on.

A major reason you might have had difficulty writing these letters is because of hidden and somewhat distorted perceptions of God's character. These misperceptions block our ability to conceive of Him as our Best Friend or Perfect Father. Because most of us hold one or more of these, I wish to talk about them in some depth.

We may think we know who God is because of what we know from the Bible. However, life experiences and what we have been taught can affect how we view God. For example, if we received accurate but one-dimensional teaching that leads us to view God solely as an almighty, sovereign Lord, we will have difficulty writing a letter speculating on His response as a Good Friend. Or if we grew up with an earthly father whose parenting was distant, unemotional, and largely absent, or, even worse, a father who was mean and demeaning, we will find it difficult to speculate on what God might say as a loving, kind, generous, present, accepting Father.

These largely hidden misperceptions affect what we "expect" God to say to us. We can't speculate as I have directed because, underneath, we are *really* expecting God to say, "How many times are we going to go over this?" Or, "Why can't you be more like my other kids who have it together?" Many of us may have heard such things from our earthly parents. Unfortunately, we kind of expect God to say something similar.

Since most of us have misconceptions of God, try to list any you may hold (see the list below for help). The sooner we identify these, the sooner God can help us begin to correct these faulty views.

Common Misperceptions about God

Note that there are elements of truth in many of these. However, they are also distorted enough that they will block our ability to talk with God as our good and perfect Father and Friend.

❖ God uses hardships and trials to teach me things. If I learn some-thing, that's good. If I don't get it, I will repeat similar scenarios until I get it right.

❖ Goes and is there for the poor, the weak, and the oppressed. I don't have any "real" problems. Therefore I should not expect much of His attention or time.

❖ God's standards are high—and rightly so. He wants me to behave, which I seem to have a hard time doing. Talking to Him means hav-ing to review what I'm doing wrong. It's up to me to get things right.

❖ God wishes I would be appreciative of all He has done for me and just be joyful and obedient. He is rightfully frustrated with me being so messed up and needy.

❖ God has already shown me what He wants; His commands are all over the Bible. I shouldn't be asking Him for anything more when I already know what He wants from me. Since I don't do what He asks me to do—pray, read my Bible, go to church, witness, serve others—how can I expect much from Him?

❖ God loves me (I suspect); He just doesn't like me.

❖ God has forgiven me, but if I do something I know is wrong, I must do penance and clean myself up before I can come to Him and be close to Him again.

❖ God doesn't have much use for me. Because of the magnitude of my past sin(s), I cannot expect God to bless me or use me.

❖ God wasn't there for me when I really needed Him. I can't depend upon Him, therefore what's the use in getting close to Him now.

❖ God is most happy with me when I'm working for Him and serving others.

   ❖ God created people and gave them good minds. Now I'm supposed to use the mind God gave me and do what I know is right. Closeness (or intimacy) with God are concepts made up by touchy/feely people.

   ❖ God loves me so much that He would never let really bad things happen to me. He wants me to be happy. Because He wants the best for me, my life will be blessed and worry free.

   ❖ God is almighty and sovereign. If I talk to Him as if He is just my father or friend, I will be irreverent and flippant.

3. Follow-up Exercise: Getting past a misconception. You may have identified some misconceptions you didn't know you held or had never put into words. One of the things this course will do is allow God to begin to recalibrate your view of Him so that your perception matches how He reveals Himself to us in the Bible. This will happen over time. For now, however, I wish to give you a simple way to set aside your misconceptions as you begin talking with God.

When speculating on how God would respond, some people find it helpful to go ahead and write a letter based on what they are convinced God is going to say—no matter how skewed that perception may be. This helps expose the misperception. When they have to write out and then read what is actually in their heads, most people can see it is not really what they want to believe about God. They can then set that letter aside and write a more genuine speculation letter.

This greatly helps in transitioning to an accurate view of God. Their "false" speculation letter might sound like this:

Dear John,

Well, I see you are finally going to pray. It is about time. You should have done that a long time ago. No wonder you are in such a mess. You need to shape up and start doing what you know you should.

Love, God

The great news is that this is not who the God of the Bible is. He can be stern and He will correct and He will command, but even then He has an amazing ability to do this such that we still feel loved. Remember, God *is* love; He can't do anything apart from love.

a. If you stalled out on speculating what God would say to you, write a letter saying exactly what you tend to think God would say to you, no matter how odd or inaccurate it seems.

b. Now that you've put words to that misconception, set that letter aside and try again on speculating what your Best Friend or Perfect Father would say. If you need help finding words that get you thinking in a new direction, use one of the following prompts to get you started.

- *Father picture.* "My son/daughter, I love you and I'm pleased you would come talk with Me. I've been waiting for the time when you would come talk with Me like this ... "

- *Friend picture.* "_____, you are My friend. I like you and I like how I made you. When you come and talk with Me, I feel happy you want to spend time with Me and let Me do life with you ... "

How to Communicate with God Using the Lord's Model Prayer

Now that we know the manner in which we should pray and how much God wants to give us Himself, that recalibrates our approach to prayer. We can share our lives with God as we would with a best friend. And we can talk as a child would talk with a perfect and loving parent. Then we also *listen* and expect—even anticipate—that God will respond to us as a best friend and as a perfect and loving father would. This is what prayer will sound and feel like.

Not only that, but God gives us Himself, in the Holy Spirit, to help us pray. Jesus said of the Holy Spirit, "He abides with you and will be in you ... the helper, the Holy Spirit, whom the Father will send in My name, He will teach you all things, and bring to your remembrance all that I said to you" (John 14:17,26, NASB). What a Father and Friend! What a privilege to be His!

Because of this promise, I now pray the Lord's Prayer very differently from how I would have prayed it in the past. I no longer simply recite it to God. Instead, I come to Him with each portion, ask specific questions, and then stop and *listen* for how my great Friend and exceptional Father wants to share with me. It is this kind of prayer—talking and listening, giving and receiving, friend-to-Friend and child-to-Parent—that communicating *with* God is all about, whether I am praying the Lord's Prayer or other prayers.

Let's look at what it is like to pray the Lord's Prayer in this manner, phrase by phrase, using the more complete version found in Matthew 6.

"OUR FATHER IN HEAVEN"

Jesus' prayer starts with the core picture of our relationship with God: "Our Father." God wants us to call Him Father with a sense of anticipation and expectation. When my granddaughter, Grace, sees me, she runs to me shouting, "Grandpa!" and she *knows* she will always see my face light up and me reaching down to pick her up and hug and kiss her; she knows I will lavish her with my love. You see, this is just who Grandpa is.

In the same way, our Heavenly Father wants us to come to Him, call out "Father," and expect to receive His delight and joy and excitement at having us with Him. This is who our God is—as astounding as it may sound. God *is* love (1 John 4:16), not just the possessor of it, and He delights in lavishing us with His parental affection. Isn't that amazing?

Even so, many people have difficulties with the concept of "Father." Today I love calling God my Father, but it hasn't always been that way. Like most of us, my relationship with my earthly father affected my view of God as my Heavenly Father.

As a young adult, I thought my dad and I were close. We both loved sports and loved watching them together. What he had to say about sports was exactly what I enjoyed talking about. I genuinely believed Dad and I were close, and calling God "Heavenly Father" was not hard for me.

However, I matured and got married and started learning about relationships and closeness and intimacy. And then I became a father.

I was in love with my daughter from the first moment I saw her. I also wanted to father her in ways unfamiliar to me; I found myself compelled to talk to her differently from anything I'd experienced with my dad. Interestingly, calling God my Father became more and more infrequent. I wasn't conscious of this; I just gradually moved from starting prayers with "Father" to using "Dear God."

I now know I was realizing things about my dad that affected my relationship with God. My dad and I *did* things together—but that was about it. I knew he loved me, but we never talked deeply. I didn't share any insecurities or fears with him, and I certainly did not share feelings about girlfriends or what it was like for me to be chosen all-tournament in basketball. My dad did not accept Jesus Christ as his Savior until late in life, so we also never talked about my faith and my relationship with God.

It took a good bit of time before I had any idea of my discomfort or confusion. Fortunately my Heavenly Father did notice and He was not pleased with this change—although my prayers were probably more in tune with how I actually saw and related to Him. Eventually He got my attention and helped me see what I was doing. Once I realized my understanding of God needed an adjustment, I was quite willing to cooperate. My relationship with my dad had caused a misperception that affected my ability to relate with my Heavenly Father in prayer.

Over the years I have come to realize I am not unique. As we talked about in the previous chapter, for most Christians, whom God is as revealed in the Bible is different from whom they think He is deep within themselves. They may talk about God in ways that are accurate to the Bible, but deep inside that is not what they truly believe. And like me, their conceptions of God have often been shaped by their earthly dads.

For example, many Christians believe—not necessarily for others but for themselves—that God is a stern father; maybe like a self-disciplined hard worker whose role is to drive His children into being the best they can be. Therefore, they expect Him to criticize what they think and feel; they rarely are doing all they should. They end up seeing life as primarily about improvement, right and wrong, and accomplishments; life is certainly not about developing relationships or doing things they might enjoy.

Others see God as a kind of grandfather who really wants them to be happy and is all about anything they want. Others see God as dangerous, someone they'd better not make mad. Still others see God as distant and hands-off; He is too busy for them. I could go on and on.

I have discovered that most Christians do not realize they hold a conception of God that varies from the Bible's clear teaching. Even if they hear or read something and suspect their conceptions of God are inaccurate, it is difficult for them to discover personal discrepancies. Therefore one of my main goals of this book is to assist readers in correcting their understanding of who God is, such that who God is in the Bible is the same as who He is deep within us.

Then when we say, "Our Father," this name will touch us deeply and be a continuous source of love and comfort and value.

"HALLOWED BE YOUR NAME"

Jesus next teaches us to say, "Hallowed be your name." How strange this phrase is to us! Hallowed means "set apart." What the Lord wants us to do is to "set apart" His Name.

We set apart the name of the Lord when we praise and adore and worship Him for *who* He is. We can do this by praising and thanking Him for His attributes and characteristics, such as love, grace, mercy, truth, sovereignty, faithfulness, and justice. We also declare and praise Him for His many names, such as the Son of God, the Son of Man, the Light of the world, the Lion of Judah, the King of kings, the Lord of lords, the Great I Am, the Way, the Truth, and the Life, and many more. (For more names, attributes, and characteristics of God, please see appendix A.)

My favorite way to set apart God's name when I pray is to follow King David's example. Years ago I read through the Bible using a wonderful tool called *The Narrated Bible*, which rearranges Scripture into the general order in which the events occurred. It was a life-changing experience to read the life of David with his psalms attached to the events that framed them. I learned that David was a *master* at identifying and claiming the specific attribute or name of God that perfectly fit the situation he faced.

If he was being falsely accused, he might claim God's truthfulness. Or if he was feeling alone or abandoned, he would apply God's presence or His faithfulness never to forsake His own. If David faced insurmountable odds, he would experience God's supremacy or supernatural power or sovereignty, declaring that He and only He is in control. I want to be like David, a man after God's own heart, a man who "tastes and sees that the Lord is good," as I declare and apply God's Name.

So in this portion of the prayer I often ask, "Father, which of your attributes or names do *You* want me to set apart today? How do you want me to know You today?" and then I listen for His response.

On a day when a situation is falling apart, He might emphasize that He is my Sovereign Father. Maybe He'll say, "Son, I know right now everything is in shambles, and you're feeling devastated, but I'm in control. I know you want to know the outcome. I know exactly what is going on, and I will reveal to you everything you need to know as you need to know it. I want to go through this with you. Nothing is going to separate you from Me in this. I'm here. I'm going to protect you. Nothing is going to be able to get to you because I am that powerful and I want to be that for you. I want to do this with you."

When I hear God say those kinds of things to me, that is Him fathering me and expressing His fatherhood to me. To hear this type of reassurance from a God who is sovereign and majestic and powerful overwhelms and humbles me and compels me to praise Him for who He is. I am in awe that Someone so majestic would still want to be my gentle and tender Father who yearns for time with me. How can these two pictures that appear to be so separate, one of majesty and one of tenderness, actually be the same God?

"YOUR KINGDOM COME"

Next Jesus teaches us that we are to pray, "Your kingdom come." For many years I rarely thought about God's kingdom and how that might relate to my everyday life. No more. I do want God's kingdom to come and rule and reign in my life, in my family, in my work, in my ministry, in my relationships, even as I play and rest.

I also want to be actively involved in God's kingdom. When I ask my Father, "How do You want Your kingdom to reign in my life today?" He has never been at a loss for words.

For example, He may show me that His priorities for today are much different from mine—will I submit to His rule? Or He may "command" a gentle response when I am furious over mistreatment—will I allow His kingdom to reign over me? Or He may say the day is to be about Him showing me He is in control at a time when chaos seems to be sovereign in my life.

His reign means His purpose and plan is working itself out in my day. When I ask Him to rule and reign, I'm likely to hear something such as, "Son, it brings Me such joy that you would want Me to do this with You. This is what I want to hear from My children. Son, you *do* want Me to rule and reign, and that delights Me."

Recently He said to me, on my wedding anniversary, that He wanted to rule and reign in how I celebrated the day with my wife. I wanted to honor Letty, and like a typical male I had some ideas of how to do that, like take her out for a great dinner.

Instead He said, "No, it's your *manner* with her I want to focus on today, not an event or something you buy her. I want you to honor her by how you treat her and talk about her and talk with her. What phrases could you use with her that would let My intentions rule here rather than yours?" That question took me far beyond what I would have thought or done or what I would have come up with.

When my Father and King reigns and rules in me, life expands. Under His rule and reign, my life becomes "bigger," but not in a way that feels heavy and burdensome and cumbersome. There's a sense of rightness to what He tells me to do. With my wife, I realized that if I celebrated with her the way my Father was directing, it would mean the world to her. At our special dinner, I ended up sharing how much she meant to me. I told her of aspects of her character that I admired and appreciated. I talked of memories that were important to me. Do I need to say how much she loved this? When God rules and reigns in me, His "ways" prevail; I continue to find this vastly superior to my ways.

"YOUR WILL BE DONE ON EARTH AS IT IS IN HEAVEN"

The prayer continues with, "Your will be done on earth as it is in heaven." Asking God what His will is for me today has been very helpful. It does me good to declare to my Father that I really do desire His will and not mine. When I think of God's will being done in heaven, that seems a given. But "His will" being done here on earth? That seems anything but the norm.

I believe each day has the potential for eternal value. The only way I can discern this potential is by asking the Lord to reveal it to me. For example, He may reveal that His will for me today is that His gentleness be seen and experienced during a meeting I am not looking forward to. Obviously that directive greatly changes my outlook and even my expectations for the meeting.

Or He may say that today is about His strength being perfected in my weakness. I can see and feel my weakness, but when I hear and receive His will that His strength is to prevail, everything seems to change. I may even feel some excitement instead of dread or fear, because I begin to anticipate how God is going to display His strength.

"GIVE US TODAY OUR DAILY BREAD"

The next portion of the Lord's model prayer is one of my favorites: "Give us today our daily bread." Many impoverished people must take this request literally. But there is another sense in which we pray this. I also need to request God's "portion" for me for today. Here is a typical way I may do this: "Father, please give me my daily bread, the portion You have personally chosen for me that will give me the life I need. Please fill me with You and with Your Living Water."

He may reply, "Watch for the trial coming today and then don't react; listen to Me and I will lead you and give you the provision you need to get through it." Or He says, "What you need today is to have some fun. Enjoy Me today and I will give you fun." On days like this, I am excited and so grateful that I chose to come to Him.

God often "feeds" me by refreshing me when I'm worn out. I come to Him spent and apathetic and unmotivated, and yet I have a lot to do. "Okay, Father," I say, "Would You take this time we have together and somehow change me so I can be what I need to be for these people I will interact with today?"

"Son," He might reply, "You *are* spent and worn. I can see that. I can see you have no energy and drive. That's because yesterday you let Me use you up. And I'm proud of you for that; you did a great job, and look at all we were able to do together. I don't see any reason we can't work together like that again today. Do you think I could do that for you today?"

"You know," I reply, "I think You could do that."

"Do you think I *could* do that or that I *will*?"

"Will. I think You will do that."

"Well, that's who I am and what I want to do with you. You delight Me and I want to give you everything you need for today. So let's do that."

"Lord, now I actually feel different! How do You do this?"

After this conversation, nothing has happened externally, yet I feel completely different and my attitude about the day has changed. It's fun for Him to get to do that with me. He finds talking like this with His kids inspiring, fulfilling, satisfying, joyful, and rewarding. He has told me so!

I am experiencing the living water I just asked for. He's experiencing the relationship He longs for with me. We both feel great satisfaction. This is the way it's supposed to work every day for every one of His kids.

"FORGIVE US OUR DEBTS AS WE ALSO HAVE FORGIVEN OUR DEBTORS"

The Lord's model prayer then reinforces the idea of "daily" with, "Forgive us our debts as we also have forgiven our debtors." In the Luke 11 prayer, this phrase is, "Forgive us our sins." Since sin is what separates us from our Father and Friend, surely we would want our sins removed as we enter into His presence.

I don't want anything to separate me from the Lord God, plus I hate being duped or tricked. I want to know what is wrong with me. I don't want to continue in patterns that others may see but I can't. I wouldn't want others saying such things as, "That Buddy sure is an angry guy." Or, "He drains the life out of you doesn't he?" Or, "He sure likes to talk about himself." Or, "Do you think he is capable of telling the truth?" Therefore, I ask my Heavenly Father to show me what I need to confess to Him that I couldn't see on my own.

Imagine one of your children asking you, "Dad/Mom, I think there are things in my life right now that aren't right, but I am not sure. Would you tell me what you see?" I fully realize this is an imaginary situation! However, if our children humbly came asking us to share what we see, how could any good parent withhold that information? In the same way, our Heavenly Father wishes us to be like Him. He desires us to be holy and righteous, not handcuffed and imprisoned by our sins. If we ask our Father to share what He sees, He will lovingly, graciously, and gently reveal our sins, even those we are not fully conscious of. He will set us free!

When I first starting asking Him to show me the sins I need to confess and what I needed to see, I did so with great hesitation. I think I expected to be flooded, overwhelmed, and filled with shame. What I did not consider is that our Father is a perfect Father. He knows our limits and He knows the perfect way to draw us to Him and to the light. His goal in correction is that we might experience life and restoration. When He corrects me, most times I do feel guilt and sometimes I feel shame over disobeying or hurting my Father, but feeling deep shame and guilt and leaving His presence feeling awful? This just does not happen. Here is what still astounds me every time God the Holy Spirit convicts me of my sin: I feel *loved*!

How can that be? How can God convict and discipline me and yet always cause me to feel loved? It truly is a mystery that is beyond me, but it's a perplexity that I rejoice in and that compels me to worship Him. When I come to the Lord I am fully aware I have no way to deal with my sins; this humbles me as I come. He is always faithful to show me what I cannot see and then graciously and mercifully wash me and cleanse me. His *living* water never fails! Praise Him!

"LEAD US NOT INTO TEMPTATION BUT DELIVER US FROM THE EVIL ONE."

The last request is, "And lead us not into temptation, but deliver us from the evil one." Imagine one of our children asking, "Dad/Mom, I think you might know how I am going to be tempted today. If you do, would you tell me how you think I might be tempted?" If we knew, there is no way we would ever withhold the knowledge of this important vulnerability. I suspect we might even have a few words of encouragement and suggestions to assist in protecting our children.

Our Heavenly Father is omniscient—He knows *everything*! He knows how each one of His children will be tempted each and every day. He desires us not to be deceived, not to sin, and not to fall for a temptation.

As I have learned to ask Him, "Father, how will I be tempted today?" I am astounded by all He shares with me: "Son, you'll be tempted to get angry today; watch your temper." Or, "Remember what I have taught you about mistreatment. Do not react when you're tempted to do so." Or, "This is going to be a tough day. Watch out for the sense of entitlement and temptation to indulge that you will feel at the end of the day."

A conversation like this does not guarantee sinlessness, nor does it guarantee holiness, but it does do a wonderful job of dealing with lots of deception. The same is true of "deliver us from the evil one." Here our Father has taught me to ask, "What schemes of the evil one do You wish me to know about? Please reveal what I need to see so I don't take his bait or walk into his trap today."

Imagine how powerful these two questions would be for our teenagers in this very difficult world in which they are trying to grow up. I am so grateful when the Lord warns, "Watch what you say to _____ today," or "You know how you get when you're annoyed with distractions. Be very careful today," or "Be cautious today when people are asking you to commit to a project."

I am so impressed with how thorough is our Father's care and protection for us. He is truly our strength and our shield.

DAILY RELATIONSHIP

I now pray Jesus' model prayer every day. It's simple, just God and me talking about these areas. I'm not praying by rote; I'm pausing as I pray, knowing God might want to say something to me about one part of the prayer or another. He might interject in the middle, He might wait to the end, He might point out a particular portion. Sometimes it's immediate; sometimes He shows me something as we go through the day. But He always does respond. Sometimes I communicate with Him in writing, sometimes not.

The point is: There isn't a prescription. As you begin to pray according to Jesus' lesson, ask God how He wants these things to work in relationship with you. Jesus' two pictures of Father and Friend show us that God wants us to come to Him, He wants us to pray, He wants us to ask—and He wants to relate with us and give us Himself. Jesus' model prayer shows us the kind of things He wants to talk with us about.

When we pray as Jesus taught us, we're obeying Jesus and honoring Him and bringing glory to Him by doing exactly what He said. His model prayer gives us a kingdom mindset if we do it every day. It enables us to start the day clean. It emphasizes dependence on Him, because we realize we don't have what we need for the day and we don't know what we need to know. Asking God these questions and listening to His responses keep us from temptations we may otherwise have blindly fallen into; it sabotages Satan's attacks and greatly diminishes his ability to deceive us.

But mostly, when I pray this way, it ensures I'm following God and His plan and will for my day. It keeps me close to Him and connected with my Father and Friend.

Practice Session

Skills You're Acquiring and Practicing

- Using Jesus' model prayer, talking with God in the manner He desires (Father and Friend), and expecting God to give you Himself in response
- Relating with God as He truly is by anticipating His affection and recalibrating your perceptions of Him

Your Assignment

Write another set of letters.

In your first letter, again talk with the Lord about things you wish to share with Him. You might use one of the topics from the Lord's Prayer. (Still avoid painful and highly difficult topics.)

In your second letter, speculate on how He would respond.

This time, make certain you anticipate your Father's affection. Since He is love, He will not communicate in a way that is not loving, even when He corrects. Our Heavenly Father is a master at parental affection.

When you write the speculation letter from God, ask yourself, "What kind of affection would a perfect Father express to a dearly loved child who said what I just said? What words would He use? How would He show His kindness, affection, attention, and delight at talking with me?" Then, put words and phrases of those kinds into your letter.

When your Father communicates with you, you will feel ...

Incredibly understood	Important	Supported
	Encouraged	Accepted
Loved	Comforted	Respected
Cared for	Affirmed	Secure
Valued	Appreciated	

Pointers

- *Friend and Father.* Use the friend and father pictures. You might picture yourself talking with your best friend. You'd be comfortable, relaxed, assured of being heard and accepted and liked. You wouldn't have to choose or guard what you say. Write to God out of that mode.

  Or, imagine what you would say if your child or niece or nephew wrote a letter to you like the one you have just written to God. If you were in a good place, how would you respond?

- *How to get "unstuck."* If you're getting stuck on how to speculate God's letter to you, remember that you can first write a letter of how you tend to expect God to react; this helps address misconceptions about God.

  Another way to get "unstuck" is to switch to a different picture (for example, if "Father" is hard, switch to "Friend").

- *Simple and specific.* Writing about specific situations and concerns will help if you're wondering whether you might be hearing God.

Sample: Here is a sample of what your letters might sound like.

Dear God,

Father, I am intrigued with this teaching on the Lord's Prayer. I have never thought about praying like described in this chapter and I am not sure how I feel about it right now. But it can't hurt to try, so here goes. I think I want to try the kingdom part.

I am not sure what I should do about Jane. I know she has problems sitting still and not talking. Most kids do, don't they? But we got that report about her from her teacher—and that seems like more of a problem than kids have at her age. I am willing to have her tested, but that would cost a bunch of money and I wonder how that would make her feel. I don't want her to think that she is weird, like I did when I was her age.

I know I have to do something, but I sure don't want to make things worse. Also if I am honest—which I guess would be foolish not to be since you already know—I'm embarrassed. This problem makes it seem like I am not a good parent.

Father I do want your kingdom to rule and reign in my life today. I just have never thought about this before. How would You want this to happen today, especially as a parent?

Casey

Dear Casey,

I like you doing these letters with Me. I know this is a stretch for you and I like you trusting Me like this. I do want My followers to pray the Lord's Prayer. It is not just a model.

On Jane, I can see that you are concerned and troubled. Any parent who cares about his children would be concerned with a report from the teacher. I am proud that your first thought was concern for her, not just anger. That is a good parent's heart.

Today My kingdom coming and My will for you is to adopt My thoughts and approach toward Jane. Casey, the main thing here is that Jane is not disrespectful or rebellious. She is full of energy and not shy. She is a delight to Me and I know she keeps things hopping at home. It is more a self-control problem. I appreciate that you want to be careful over what you do here and not traumatize this sweet girl. That is using good judgment and sensitivity.

I understand that you are embarrassed and think this reflects on you, but you are a good parent. You and Lee have done a good job and the teacher is not thinking negatively of you; she is used to these types of problems.

There is no need for testing now. Best is for you and Lee to sit down and calmly talk to her. Let's come up with a reward system to use and make a chart with some stars; she likes stars. Obviously pray with her.

Communicate confidence that I am going to help her and that you and Lee believe she will be able to learn how to sit more still and not talk. Let her know how much you two love her. I will give you and Lee words to speak to her tonight. By doing this you are allowing me to rule over you. By the way, I will help you with this. You know how concerned you are for Jane and how much you want to take care of her? That is how concerned I am for you and how you are feeling and doing with all this. You could not possibly love her more than I love you.

Love, God

Follow-up Coaching

If you have not yet written your letters, please do so before you read and work through this coaching portion.

If you're like many people I've worked with, you may be concerned about whether you "got it right." That is not my top concern for you at this time. I simply want you to *do* it. I've worked with God enough to know that if His children just come to Him, He is committed to coach and correct and help them, just like a father would help a kid learn to walk or to talk.

You may also wonder why I'm having you write letters. Letter writing enables us to express ourselves well. It helps underdeveloped thoughts and words become clear. It offers a practical way to review and to see growth.

Letter writing is also a form of meditating. We are to meditate on the Word of God and God Himself. When we have to speculate on what God would say to us, writing that letter enables us to concentrate intently on who God is. As we do this, we can progress in our thinking and in our understanding, plus we give God more focused opportunity to lead us deeper.

In this coaching section, I want to focus on the letters you are writing speculating how God would respond to you.

1. God wants to help you communicate with Him—for sure He does not want you to do this on your own. One of the Holy Spirit's ministries to you is to "guide you into all truth" (John 16:13). Look back at your speculation letter of what God would say and ask Him, "Would You please show me anything here that's not accurate about You or what You would say? And would You show me whatever else I need to see that I wouldn't notice without Your help?"

Does God highlight anything that's not what He is saying to you? Does He point out anything else He wants you to notice or impress upon you something that is especially accurate? In your notebook, write down what you see and what God says to you.

2. God's affection. Were you able to include God's affection in the speculation letter you wrote on His behalf? This is an essential part of who He is and therefore a normal part of His everyday interactions with you.

a. Look back to see if there is affection, according to the list I gave you in the assignment above. Underline places in your letter where you see affection.

b. If you had a difficult time finding these items, go back to your letter and write in a few affectionate phrases, remembering that you are still speculating on what God would say. Particularly pick out an area or two from the list that is difficult for you and speculate on what it might sound like if God said something to make you feel one of those things.

3. God as "Father." You may not have been raised in a loving home with mentally and relationally healthy parents. Therefore, the picture of a perfectly loving father or parent is difficult even to imagine. I can relate to this, because I was not raised in a Christian home and my parents were not mentally healthy.

However, the Lord has used my experience as a father to begin to recalibrate my understanding of Him as my Father. When my daughter was born, I was deeply touched the moment I saw her in the delivery room. The Lord opened up emotions and paternal instincts that were foreign to me. Shortly after her birth I began to think about how I would respond if my daughter shared with me some of the things I shared with God. If I, as imperfect as I am, would feel deep love and emotion for my daughter and want to respond to her out of that love, how much more would my perfect Heavenly Father feel love and caring for me?

If you have a child or grandchild you adore, consider using that understanding to help you meditate on God's response to you. (If you have no children, think of a child who looks up to you and whom you have a special affection for.) If your child said the things to you that you are sharing with God and if you were in a loving and healthy parenting mode, how would you respond? This is a taste of how your Heavenly Father wants to respond to you.

If you were blocked by an inability to relate with God as Father, write another speculation letter with these points in mind, and see if it is helpful.

THE BIBLICAL BASIS FOR RELATIONAL COMMUNICATION WITH GOD

I shared with you the relational pictures from Luke 11 and how I've experienced them in the Lord's Prayer, but you might think, *That is just one passage. Does God really want to relate to me and speak directly to me like this?*

My Christian background is conservative evangelical. I believe in the inerrancy of Scripture and the supremacy of the Word of God. I graduated from a seminary known as one of the elite in training people to study and teach the Bible. I am committed to letting the Bible speak for itself rather than attempting to show how Scripture could be interpreted to support a certain teaching or theology.

I say all this for a point: The Bible must speak of this concept of communicating *with* God and listening to Him in order for this approach to prayer to be biblical and accurate. When we study the breadth of Scripture we discover that the relational pictures in Luke 11 rest upon a foundation of God consistently expressing His desire for an interactive, intimate relationship with us.

The father and friend pictures in Luke 11 flow from God's intense desire to share His nature, His life, His wisdom, and His words with us, if we will only come and ask. God's desire to communicate with us and live in close communion with us is found throughout Scripture. I am going to share from many of these passages (in appendix B you'll find many more verses that I believe teach and model or refer to these concepts).

GOD ACTIVELY LIVES WITH US

In light of the close relationship God wants with us, consider again the amazing thing He's done in giving us the gift of Himself through the Holy Spirit. When we accept the Lord Jesus Christ as our Savior, God desires for us to know that we are His, that He now lives within us, and that He desires a oneness with us that is unparalleled among our relationships.

Ponder for a moment the incredible ministry of God the Holy Spirit, who lives within us. He

Regenerates us from a state of death into life (Titus 3:5)
Baptizes us into the body of Christ (1 Corinthians 12:13)
Indwells us (John 14:17)
Sanctifies us to become like Christ (1 Peter 1:2)
Fills us (Ephesians 5:18)
Seals us (Ephesians 1:13)
Teaches us (John 14:26)
Illuminates the Word of God and truth (Ephesians 1:17-18)
Gifts us (1 Corinthians 12:11)
Leads us (Galatians 5:18)
Anoints us (1 John 2:20)
Convicts of sin (John 16:8)
Restrains sin (2 Thessalonians 2:6-8)
Guides us into all truth (John 16:3)
Intercedes for us (Romans 8:16)

Assures us we are God's children (Romans 8:16)

Appoints us to specific service (Acts 13:2)

Communicates God's love to us (Romans 5:5)

Connects us with the Father (Galatians 4:6)

Testifies to us about Jesus (John 15:26)

Makes the Father's thoughts known to us (John 16:14-15)

No wonder Jesus said to His disciples, "But I tell you the truth, it is to your advantage that I go away; for if I do not go away, the Helper will not come to you; but if I go, I will send Him to you" (John 16:7, NASB). Yet many of us experience very few of these incredible benefits. We are often like the man in one of the Communicating with God courses. He silently read over this list of what the Holy Spirit does and then said with sadness in his voice, "You know, I think the only thing on here that I really know about is the Holy Spirit convicting me of sin."

Do you begin to see what we are missing when we do not realize the extent to which God is present and active in our lives? The Father's intense desire to do life with us is why the Lord God commands us to

Be led by the Spirit (Romans 8:14)

Pray in the Spirit (Ephesians 6:18)

Live by the Spirit (Galatians 5:16)

Keep in step with the Spirit (Galatians 5:25)

I believe that while I am still here on earth I will never be able to fully grasp the significance of the Lord God giving us Himself in the Holy Spirit. Let's look at just a few passages that show what God desires for us as He lives in us.

GOD DESIRES ONENESS WITH US

Given the immensity of the gift God has given us by coming to live with us through the Holy Spirit, it should not surprise us that He desires far more than a casual or distant connection with us. Even so, the level of intimacy the Lord desires when He talks of wanting "oneness" with us is difficult to grasp.

The night before He died, Jesus openly expressed this desire for connection: "Remain in me, and I will remain in you ... I am the vine; you are the branches ... apart from me you can do nothing" (John 15:4-5). Listen to His words about oneness later that night, in what we call His high priestly prayer. This is what He is praying for you and me:

> That all of them may be one, Father, just as you are in me and I am in you. May they also be in us so that the world may believe that you have sent me. I have given them the glory that you gave me, that they may be one as we are one. I in them and you in me. May they be brought to complete unity to let the world know that you sent me and have loved them even as you have loved me. (John 17:21-23)

This "oneness" truly is beyond us; Jesus in me and me in Him. This potential for oneness speaks of an intimacy that is unparalleled in any other relationship. It is only somewhat experienced in the relationship between a husband and wife where, as Jesus said, "The two will become one flesh. So they are no longer two, but one" (Mark 10:8).

This oneness is where we share ourselves deeply with Him in vulnerability and trust, and He receives what we share and gives us love and understanding. Oneness is also where He shares His heart and the essence of who He is along with many of His secrets, and we are able to receive what He shares with us and give Him our love and understanding.

GOD DESIRES TO SHARE HIS THOUGHTS WITH US

Part of this oneness is that God shares His thoughts and wisdom with us when we come to Him and ask. One of my favorite verses is

Proverbs 2:6: "For the LORD gives wisdom, and from his _____ come knowledge and understanding." I've left out a word. What would you guess it is?

When I've asked others that question, most people guess, "From God's Word" come knowledge and understanding (that is what I would have guessed). Others guess "grace" or "faithfulness." Actually, the verse says, "from His *mouth* come knowledge and understanding." God wants to speak His thoughts with us. Look at God's promise in the whole passage:

> My son, if you accept my words and store up my commands within you, turning your ear to wisdom and applying your heart to understanding, and if you call out for insight and cry aloud for understanding, and if you look for it as for silver and search for it as for hidden treasure, *then you will understand the fear of the* LORD *and find the knowledge of God.*
>
> For the LORD gives wisdom, and from his *mouth* come knowledge and understanding.... Then you will understand what is right and just and fair—every good path. For wisdom will enter your heart, and knowledge will be pleasant to your soul. (verses 1-6, 9-10, emphasis added)

Notice what we are to do: turn our ears, apply our hearts, call out, cry aloud, look, search ... doesn't that sound like Luke 11? When we do, the Lord promises us that we'll understand what it means to fear Him and we'll find His knowledge. How does it come? From his *mouth*.

When I first studied this verse and contemplated it with the Lord, I wondered why He chose the word *mouth*. It doesn't seem to be how most Christians acquire wisdom. Knowing that the Lord carefully chooses each word in the Holy Scriptures, I knew this word wasn't accidental. I believe God chose the word *mouth* because He desires to personally teach and dispense wisdom to each of His children in a relational way. His gift of Himself makes that possible.

In Jeremiah 33:3 (NASB) the Lord God says, "Call to Me and I will answer you, and I will tell you great and mighty things, which you do not know." The truth is, any time God speaks to us He is revealing things from His great and mighty store of wisdom that we do not know. It's God's good heart to share Himself with us. James promises us that if we lack wisdom, we should "ask God, who gives generously to all without finding fault" (James 1:5).

Again, notice in Jeremiah 33 how relational God is and how personal. He invites us to call and ask and come to Him. He is saying, "I will come live with you and tell you things out of the depths of My wisdom and understanding." As I have claimed this promise and "called" out to Him countless times, I have been astounded by all He will show me.

When the Holy Spirit comes to live in oneness with us and shares God's thoughts with us, it is little wonder that God also wants us to begin to *experience* His presence with us.

GOD WANTS US TO EXPERIENCE HIS PRESENCE

Psalm 23 has comforted God's people for centuries with its amazing picture of how personally our Shepherd cares for us. David beautifully teaches us from Psalm 23:4, "Even though I walk through the valley of the shadow of death, I will fear no evil, for you are with me." In the past, if you had asked me why I should not fear even at the thought of our greatest foe, death, I would have said, "Well, I will not fear because the Bible is planted in my heart," or maybe, "Because God has proven Himself faithful to me." But this is not what the man after God's own heart says. He says, "I will fear no evil for *you* are with me." I love this truth! Experiencing God's presence is His desire for us.

Being a pastor, I have been with a number of people when they died. I've observed that for almost everyone, Christian and non-Christian, the "valley of the shadow of death" is unsettling and frightening. This is the point when death is inevitable, but it is not quite here. In the valley, fear seems unavoidable.

But what I have found fascinating and extremely assuring is that when death itself approaches, Christians who know Jesus *experientially* do not fear. Isn't that impressive? David gives us the reason: because the Lord God Himself is with us, relationally and experientially, not just cognitively or intellectually. The one who knows how to come into the presence of the Lord and listen to His comforting, parental voice "fears no evil."

I think of it like this. Back in the early days of the Dallas Cowboys there was a mountain of a man named Bob Lilly. He was one of the greatest linemen of all time and no one—I mean *no one*—messed with Bob Lilly. Imagine if you or I were alone with Bob Lilly in his prime; it is night and we come to a dark street corner. Suddenly three tough looking men are approaching. My heart would be racing.

But imagine Bob Lilly pushing me behind him and saying, "Westbrook, you just stay behind me. I've got this situation covered. Actually you just watch; this will be fun. No one is going to mess with us." My heart would still be pounding, but I'd have a different feeling— a sense of anticipation and a peace in the midst of some remaining anxiety. But no fear.

Now imagine if Bob were with me, but slightly *behind* me. The three men approach and I put my hand behind me ... and cannot feel him. I say, "Bob ...?" and get no answer. I am not experiencing Bob's presence. I might *think* he is there, but it's not the same at all, and fear would overtake me.

Similarly, the reason we do not fear anything, even death, is not just because the Bible is planted in our hearts or because of our faith or even because of God's past faithfulness. We do not fear because the Lord God is *with* us relationally and experientially—we listen to Him speak; this is not just some spiritual truism.

GOD WANTS US TO KNOW HIS VOICE

God has a longing and expectation for us to know His voice as we follow

Him, not just in the valley of the shadow of death, but in all of life. I love what Jesus tells us in John 10:27: "My sheep listen to my voice; I know them, and they follow me." Jesus said, "My sheep *listen* to my voice." What a promise and what an invitation! And notice, it is after hearing and recognizing His voice that Jesus expects us to follow Him.

This passage also reassures us about the question we all ask, "How can I really know I'm hearing Him and not making something up?" Our Good Shepherd (who knows how foolish and incapable sheep are) promises that we *will* know His voice when we hear it. Jesus is on our side in wanting to make sure we hear Him clearly and accurately. His Spirit, the *Holy* Spirit, the Spirit of truth, indwells us and has a vested interest in protecting us from all evil, all deception, and even all human craziness.

GOD WANTS TO REVEAL HIMSELF
TO THOSE WHO TRULY DESIRE TO LISTEN

We have a God who *wants* to reveal Himself to those who truly want Him and what He has to say. Listen to Jesus in Luke 8:16-18:

> No one lights a lamp and then covers it with a bowl or hides it under a bed. A lamp is placed on a stand, where its light can be seen by all who enter the house. For all that is secret will eventually be brought into the open, and everything that is concealed will be brought to light and made known to all. So pay attention to *how you hear*. To those who *listen to my teaching*, more understanding will be given. But for those who are not *listening*, even what they think they understand will be taken away from them. (NLT, emphasis added)

These verses come at the very end of Jesus' explanation to His disciples of the parable of the sower and the seed. He is saying that not everyone who hears Him really *hears*. In fact, Jesus had ended the parable by calling out (as God does so often in Scripture), "He who has ears to hear, let him hear" (8:8, NASB).

Notice that He doesn't say, "He that has eyes to read, let Him *read* My law and the prophets." He doesn't say, "He that has a mind to understand, let him understand My theological precepts and concepts." Instead, Jesus says, "He that has ears to hear, let him *hear.*"

Jesus is teaching that God will reveal Himself in a very relational way, in contrast to a cognitive, researched way. God is going to disclose things that are precious to Him. He is saying, "The closer you get to Me the more I have to share with you. I desire to be known and to reveal Myself to you, even My secrets. But I seek people who will faithfully pursue Me and come to Me and *heed* what I am saying." God is saying, "If you choose to listen to Me, I will give you more understanding. I will communicate. You will listen, you will hear, I will help you understand. If you don't *hear* in this fashion, then you will lose the little understanding that you have." May we *listen and hear* the Lord God as He reveals Himself and teaches us His truth.

A GOD WHO COMMUNICATES

When these passages are taken together, to me they paint the picture of the relationship God desires with His children and the process He uses with them.

Many years ago, God gave me a real-life picture of what this looks like. I attended a conference where Dr. Richard Halverson, then Chaplain of the United States Senate, spoke. To this day I have never seen the Lord Jesus Christ so visible in a man. He clearly *loved* Jesus in a way that was new to me. On several occasions he would be teaching the Word of God and break out in song. At first this shocked me and made me uncomfortable; I didn't know what to think. But it became obvious that he was not "performing." He just couldn't help himself; he was overtaken with the Lord as he spoke about Him.

At the end of the week I mustered up all my courage and said to him, "Dr. Halverson, I have never seen the Lord Jesus Christ so visible in a person like I see in you. I have a request. Could I spend a few days with you? I'd just like to follow you around. I'm not asking you to teach me anything or show me anything, I just want to watch you. I think the Lord has shown me that He has something for me to see as I watch you in everyday life."

Dr. Halverson looked at me and paused before responding. Then he said, "Let me give you my card. Write to my assistant and tell him what you told me." That was it. He was polite and gracious, but I felt this was probably his gentle way of saying, "I am the chaplain of the United States Senate. Son, do you have any idea what you are asking?" But I felt I had done what God wanted me to.

A couple of months later I was going through the mail only to find a letter from him! He invited me to come and gave me two dates to choose from. I was so excited. When the day came and I got to be with him, I am not sure even then he fully grasped what I was asking. He graciously allowed me to be with him and showed me several off-the-tourist-track places in the Capitol and Senate chambers.

But here is what happened that I will never forget. As we walked the halls of the Capitol or entered the Senate dining room, and he would be approaching a senator, *every time* he would talk with the Lord in a slight whisper. He asked very specific questions. By the way he then addressed the senator, it was clear to me he had heard a response from the Lord.

As I watched him over these two days, what astounded me was that he was unwilling to do anything or talk to anyone without first talking *with* the Lord. Here was a man experiencing unparalleled closeness with God. He did seem "one" with the Lord.

Dr. Halverson redefined maturity in Christ for me. To most of us, maturity means becoming independent and capable of taking care of ourselves, like the maturity we all hope will eventually happen with our children. Dr. Halverson taught me that spiritual maturity means becoming increasingly dependent—dependent upon the Lord Jesus Christ and Him alone.

I wanted what Dr. Halverson experienced: this closeness, to hear and know Jesus' voice, to have God share His thoughts and even secrets with me. I still thank and praise God for showing me a man who mastered communicating *with* God in everyday life.

The Lord God has made it clear that He wishes this closeness with each of us, a "oneness" as He says it, that is unique among all relationships. He yearns for us to communicate *with* Him, pour out our hearts and share ourselves with Him. And He yearns to communicate with us. He calls us to come and listen. He imparts wisdom through His mouth. Jesus claims we will listen to His voice.

In the next chapter we'll begin to talk about what it is like to hear God and begin to engage in conversation with Him, so we can open the door to this relationship. Let's allow God to fully be who He is, and let's allow Him to declare what prayer is to be.

Practice Session

Skills You're Acquiring and Practicing

- Anticipating that your Father and Friend wants to relate and communicate personally with you
- Tuning in to His thoughts toward you
- Listening for God's affection

Your Assignment

Please continue practicing with another set of letters, one from you to God and then a response from Him to you.

In your letter, speak to the Lord about something that is on your mind, something that is bothering you to some extent. Ask Him to assist you in hearing from Him.

As you write "His" letter, speculate on what you think He would say in response to what you are sharing.

Pointers

- *Anticipate God's affection.* Because you are writing to your Father and anticipating His response, please continue to anticipate His affection. For example, when we share difficulties and struggles with Him, He gives outstanding understanding and compassion as a wonderful father would. Please make sure you include this when you speculate on how He would respond.

- *Allow God to participate.* Practice tuning in to what God may be saying to you. When you're writing God's response letter, ask yourself, "How would a perfect parent or best friend respond to what I've just said?" Then, using that frame of reference, ask, "Father/Friend, would You speak to me like that?" And begin writing your letter.

  In essence you're saying, "God, would You do this with me? I'm going to start writing, and I'm not going to worry about whether it's You or me."

- *If you think in pictures.* Use a scene or "picture" to help you, if you're more visually oriented. Sometimes people find it help to picture themselves talking with God in a specific setting, such as by the stream spoken of in Psalm 23 or perhaps while sitting together in a quiet place. See appendix D for more information.

Sample: Here is a sample of what your letters might sound like.

Dear God,

I do want to praise You for who You are. I do praise You for Your omnipotence. Your great power has meant so much to me. As you know, I love the mountains. It is hard for me to imagine even thinking up mountains for the first time and then designing them. I think You did wonderful work. I also am grateful for how powerful You are in my life.

Today I want to talk to you about my neighbor. What got me to thinking about him is the stuff on forgiveness. He sure bothers me. I don't understand how anyone can live like that. His yard is a disaster and it makes the neighborhood look crummy.

And I don't think I have ever seen him without a beer and a cigarette. I don't like how he talks with our kids and I sure don't like his language. Then he complains about our dog and our dog is a great dog.

Anyway I just don't like him and don't trust him. We have such a great neighborhood except for Bill. I know You are going to say I have a bad attitude, and I probably do. So help me with my attitude. And I guess I will go ahead and pray for him. I would sure love it if You got hold of Him and cleaned up his act.

Okay, enough for now. Thanks for listening.

Love, Alex

P.S. How are You feeling about me and and the letters I'm writing to You?

Dear Alex,

First, I love it that you are truly desiring to communicate with Me. As your Father this is what I most want. I am really pleased that you have written to Me. And it isn't so bad is it? I appreciate your praise of My mountains. I really do like mountains and I enjoy sharing them with you.

Bill is something else. I know he is hard for you and I understand why. You are correct, he really is not a good neighbor and he is rude to the kids and pretty much everyone else. He has had a hard life and, yes, he has brought a lot on himself.

I was impressed that you did pray for him. I know it will not be a surprise to you that he hasn't had many pray for him. Alex, you are a good man and you are one of My sons. I really do care for Bill and I love him. He is a mess, but I still love him.

I am proud of you for coming to Me and talking to Me about this. I would like for you to continue to pray for Bill and ask Me to soften your heart to him. I know you feel that he is hopeless, but as you said, I am omnipotent.

Please show him some kindness and don't react so quickly when he is himself—I want your kids to get to watch how you treat him. I want them to love all that I have created and not look down on those who are different from them. I have not given up on Bill. Let's talk again soon.

Love, God

Follow-up Coaching

Remember that communicating with God is something you do, not something you read about. Please take the time to write your letters before continuing.

1. Key indicators. As you write your letters to God, you're doing well if you are

❑ Telling God what you think and feel about the topic, not just the facts about the topic

❑ Writing more in depth about one topic rather than writing about a list of topics or writing generally

❑ Talking as you would if you were talking with a good friend or very good parent

❑ Taking the risk of speaking with God as if He really is personal, available, interested, affectionate, and involved with you.

How are you doing in these areas? Write down your evaluation (ask God to help you see this from His viewpoint).

2. God speaks specifically and personally. As you write the letters "from" God, are you speculating on God's replies to what you're *actually* saying? Remember that God is your perfect parent. He knows *you* and will want to reply to you specifically.

Here's an example. Your company is being restructured and you're being assigned to a new department. You write to God about how you feel like you're losing the good job situation you've enjoyed for the past five years.

Consider the following two responses that you might speculate from God.

> *Example one:* "Don't be afraid. Remember that I love you. I can bring good from any situation."

> *Example two:* "Child, it's not easy when something that has been going well is shaken up, isn't it? I know how much this reminds you of other changes that have been sprung on you. You're feeling disregarded. But I saw this coming, and I knew

how it would affect you. I have much I want to give you in the middle of this. I'd be so pleased if you would let Me be part of it with you."

Example one is a good start. But a perfect parent or incredible friend is going to talk with you about *your* concerns, as in example two.

Principle: When you speculate on what God might say, be sure to respond specifically to what you wrote in your letter. If there is a place of great pain, God will respond to it. If you're happy about something, God will share your happiness. If you worship and praise Him, He will receive it from you.

Look back at God's letter to you. If it was very general, take another stab at it. Let God *relate* with you. Ask Him to help you hear and access His affection, specific wisdom, and care for you. Write a new letter in your course notebook.

3. God as He truly is. In our culture, we are encouraged to move toward success, independence, security, strength, health, and financial well-being. We may have been raised by parents who told us, "I just want you to be happy." Sometimes, we bring these cultural values into our expectations of what life with God will be like.

Think back over the letters you've written speculating on how God would respond to you. Do you attribute to Him statements like any of the following?

- "I always want you to be valued."

- "I want you to succeed."

- "I never want you to feel tired."

- "I just want you to be happy."

- "I don't want you to hurt or experience pain."

- "I want you to feel confident."

There may be some truth in these statements. However, many bypass a key truth: God does not promise to shield us from difficulty, struggles, and pain. He will allow us to experience failure, heartache, weariness, doubt, sickness, unhappiness, weakness, loss, and rejection—actually, these are part of His overall plan for His kids. But He will also be present with us and relate with us in the midst of them.

In your letters, underline any statements like the ones above. Then ask God, "Father, would You help me hear a more customized response from You?" Write down how you sense Him responding.

How to Engage in Conversation with God

I n the previous chapters, I've been laying a foundation that will ground you as you begin a personal, two-way dialogue with God. With that basis, I now want to talk about what hearing from God is like and how it happens.

When I ask believers, "Was there ever a time when you knew God communicated with you?" most of them say yes. Their faces light up, and they talk with excitement and enthusiasm of what happened.

As I've listened to their stories, I generally hear of times when God, out of His grace, simply broke into their consciousness in a way that works for them. Those who are visual may speak of a picture they received from the Lord. Others speak of a warning they just knew must be heeded—they had a strong sense not to be in a car or an airplane that later crashed, and they are convinced this was the Lord speaking to them. Some tell me of feeling *urged* to call a friend, not knowing he had just received a cancer diagnosis. Others talk about a clear sentence they "heard" that was undeniably the Lord, such as, "This is the man I have for you," or "This illness is serious but it will not take your life," or "Today you will receive a call that is a blessing from Me."

A good friend shared such a time with me. She had been experiencing great fatigue, which she attributed to stress. Her mother insisted she get checked out; several X rays and tests eventually revealed two masses in her lung.

A few weeks later she discovered she had been pregnant during these tests. She faced a giant dilemma: Put the baby at risk with treatment procedures that would require anesthesia and surgery, or terminate the pregnancy. Should she get the lung masses treated or should she have the baby?

Waiting for many months to treat the masses could be deadly, and she seriously considered terminating the pregnancy. Yet she chose to have the baby, believing the Lord led her to that decision. She told me her attitude was not great. The pregnancy was extremely difficult, her fatigue was much worse, and she was not very happy with God. The Lord gave her a healthy baby girl and also gave her the baby's name: Grace—which she says was a convicting irony after months of her bad attitude. Unfortunately the delivery was about as difficult as the pregnancy and required a C-section. This surgery delayed the necessary lung surgery for another three months.

Finally the time for the surgery came. During an extended time of intercessory prayer, my friend "heard" the Lord speak these words: "I will not take your entire lung, but you will be in severe pain for seven days." She was blown away. She knew this was the Lord and she was overjoyed that she would not lose her entire lung.

Sure enough, the situation went exactly as God said it would—no cancer, partial loss of her lung, and intense pain that abruptly ended after the seventh day.

She shared with me how incredible this entire event has been in her life and how God used it greatly to show her who He was. She said hearing God speak so clearly at the end of the ordeal was a special gift.

As many have shared similar stories, the common denominator is that everyone is certain God spoke and that hearing Him was a great blessing and special memory. When I ask, "Wouldn't it be great if this was a frequent experience rather than something that only happened a few times in a lifetime?" all respond with an emphatic, "Yes!"

I am convinced that our God and Father desires each and every one of His children to hear from Him on a regular basis. The reason we don't is that we haven't learned how to do it skillfully. Some people are puzzled or put off when I use the word *skillful*, as if I'm talking about some Christians who are better or more advanced than others. But I simply believe that communicating with God is a skill. Just as my wife and I learned to communicate with each other, practiced it diligently, and became good at it, so we can learn to communicate with God by practicing interacting with Him according to the instructions He gave us in Luke 11.

The first step to gaining that skill is to look more closely at *how* communicating with Him happens and what it's like to listen to Him.

CONVERSING WITH GOD

I believe communicating with God is essentially as simple as communicating with any other person: We say something and then we listen while the other person—in this case, God—replies. Then we say something in response ... and enter into a two-way dialogue in real time.

Yet because we are communicating with a Person who is Spirit, not with another human being, I find it elusive to describe precisely how this works. I am using the words *hear* and *listen*, yet I don't mean I audibly hear God's voice like I hear a friend's voice. (Some people from time to time may hear God's voice; we certainly have biblical examples of God speaking audibly; I never have experienced this.)

Generally, the Holy Spirit will "speak" to our spirits. It is more accurate to describe it as "thoughts and words from God that enter our minds." Rarely will these come in a booming tone; more typically, these thoughts and words may sound like our own voices. Yet what God says tends to be wiser than our thoughts—and definitely more righteous, loving, and thoughtful. His words impart life.

Sometimes these thoughts may come in full sentences. Sometimes they may "unroll" in your mind as you write them down. Sometimes you'll receive an impression that "downloads" a whole idea that you then put into several sentences. Sometimes you may "see" a picture with your mind's eye that the Lord then begins to explain. What is happening is that the Holy Spirit is communicating, internally, to your spirit, using the method seen in Romans 8:16: "The Spirit himself testifies with our spirit that we are God's children."

I believe you can see an example of this Spirit-to-spirit communication in 2 Chronicles 20. A massive and intimidating foreign army has come to make war on Judah. King Jehoshaphat calls all the people together, stands up in front of them and prays to God, ending his prayer with the admission, "We do not know what to do, but our eyes are upon you." In the silence after the prayer, "All the men of Judah, with their wives and little ones, stood there before the Lord."

Then "the Spirit of the Lord came upon Jahaziel ... as he stood in the assembly. He said: 'King Jehoshaphat and all who live in Judah and Jerusalem! This is what the Lord says to you: "Do not be afraid or discouraged because of this vast army. For the battle is not yours, but God's.'"

Did Jahaziel hear an audible voice in his ear as he stood there in the crowd? Did he have a vision? The passage doesn't tell us, but I believe he "heard" God's thoughts and words in his mind. This is typical and a common way God communicates with His people.

TYPICAL AND COMMON?

You might wonder that I would say God has a typical and common way of talking with us because, for many of us, hearing God in this way is neither typical nor common.

Supernatural, Not Magical

Communicating with God doesn't *feel* typical to us, mainly because it is supernatural. As students of the Bible know, the world is both natural and spiritual, and our God interacts with us in both of these dimensions. Yet some Christians are so wary of the evil and sinful part of the unseen world and are so uncomfortable with what they cannot objectively quantify, that they hold to a belief that the written Word of God is the only way God communicates with His children. In doing so, I believe they miss much of the reality of the supernatural and very personal relationship God desires to have with each and every one of His children.

I want to emphasize that while communication with God is indeed "supernatural," it is not "magical." Let me explain. Magical acts have been with mankind for generations. In the Bible we see witchcraft and sorcery, we see demons, and we see Satan. There clearly are "supernatural" forces beyond the visible, natural world we live in, but these demonic and cultic realities are not worthy of comparison to the supernatural ways of the Lord God.

Communicating with God is "supernatural" in that it occurs outside the natural world we can feel, touch, taste, and quantify. But in no way is it connecting with a magical force, nor can this means of communication be pirated by Satan and his demonic ways. As I will explain, God will teach us how to communicate with Him and He will passionately teach us how to discern and know His voice. As Jesus says, "My sheep listen to my voice; I know them, and they follow me" (John 10:27).

Why Haven't I Heard of This?

When hearing of communicating with God as being something common, many people think that surely if God were really desiring to speak with us like this, most Christians would already be doing it. After all, most of us have imagined how wonderful it would be to sit down with God and ask Him all the things that are troubling us and talk personally with Him.

My simple response to this question is that most Christians do not know this type of interaction with God is possible. They don't expect it, and therefore they don't allow time and space for it or notice when God wants to speak with them.

Think of it this way. Imagine I give you a TV and satellite TV service, but don't show you anything about it. The TV happens to be on the History Channel when I plug it in, and there it stays. What's more, I don't fiddle with the settings and make sure they are okay, so you only see things in black and white. Then one day, someone comes in, picks up your remote, changes some menus and switches channels. Suddenly, you are watching 250 channels in full color. There was nothing wrong with your TV, the channels were there all along—you just didn't know how to tune in.

Something similar happens to us in prayer and relating with God. If our Christian experience is only on one "channel," such as praying through a list or studying the Bible, we think that is the sum of life with God. We simply don't know how to access more.

Over the years, when I share the contents of Jesus' lesson plan on prayer along with practical direction on how to skillfully apply this instruction, the most common response is, "Nobody taught me how to do this." When Christians begin following these instructions, they begin to communicate *with* God and not just talk to Him.

The Silence of God

Another reason we don't expect or have confidence that God will talk with us is that we believe we have a great deal of experience with what seems like God's silence.

Sometimes we say God is "silent" when He is not responding to our prayers in the manner we're asking for. Because we rarely expect God to communicate directly and specifically in reply to our prayers, we tend to talk about God "answering" prayers when He does what we ask Him to or provides what we ask for or indicates a direction we should take. If He isn't *doing* something, we deduce He isn't answering. But just because He's not giving us something we're asking for doesn't mean He doesn't want to *speak* to us about it—or about other things in our lives. Do you see the difference? God might not *do* what we want Him to do, but He does want to *speak to His son or His daughter!*

Another take on God's silence comes from a distinct line of teaching. For many years, very credible scholars have taught about the "silence of God" as a discipline of the Christian life. This teaching says silence is one of the means the Lord uses to deepen our relationship and trust with Him.

I greatly respect these teachers and I do see validity in the concept of the silence of God, yet I do not think how this is taught, as "complete silence," is accurate. I know we are to love the Lord our God with all of our hearts, souls, minds, and strength. I know we are to trust Him more than anything or anyone else, including ourselves. I know we are "one" with Him. He lives in us and we live in Him; we are "in Christ."

And yet this teaching says that apparently we are "one" with, and love and trust deeply, someone who occasionally "disappears" on us. This would be as if I'm pouring out my soul to a friend, sharing great difficulties and burdens. I can tell he is listening, but there is zero response when I finish talking. My friend doesn't say anything and doesn't even communicate anything nonverbally.

After a few moments I ask for a response—nothing!

I ask if he heard what I just shared—nothing!

I ask what is wrong—nothing!

Yet he looks right at me; I feel certain he is listening; he just won't respond to anything I say, neither verbally nor nonverbally. Finally I realize that, for whatever reason, this is the end of the conversation and he has nothing to say. So I leave.

What's more, there are times when I want to spend time with him and cannot find him anywhere. I e-mail, call, write letters, show up at his house, try to make appointments at his office. He doesn't respond, doesn't even let me know whether he's in town. Nothing.

Let's say this does not happen often, but it happens often enough. Could I feel close to someone like this? Could I trust and feel safe in his presence, feel deeply understood? Feel eager to tell him about what I'm really thinking and feeling? I would have to say, "No way!" Yet this picture seems consistent with what some people teach about "the silence of God."

Here is my take on God's "silence": I have never yet experienced it. God has never gone mute on me or disappeared relationally. I *have* experienced (with some frequency!) God not talking to me about something I wish to talk about or Him choosing not to respond to a specific question I want answered. But here is the difference.

In my experience, our Father says something like, "Son, we are not going to talk about that." Sometimes He explains a bit, sometimes that is all He says. Sometimes He says, "I am not going to answer that question." Sometimes He communicates, "We have talked about that before and you know where I stand." Sometimes it is more like, "Son you just would not be able to understand. Remember, My ways are not your ways and My thoughts are not your thoughts," referring to Isaiah 55:8-9. At other times, He means, "You are just going to have to trust Me."

In one sense here, God *is* silent; He will not talk about what I want to talk about. I am not in charge of the conversation. But when He says He is not going to talk, that is much different from … *nothing*. I may not like or understand or agree with His response, but it feels much different from a mute, expressionless stare. And it doesn't mean He is not perfectly willing to talk with me about many, many other things.

We, at times, parent our children in much the same way. How many times has your child said, "Why not?" or, "Why can't I?" or, "But I want to!" And you respond, "We are just not going to go there," or even that familiar old saying, "Because I said so." There actually may be times you don't say a word, but most of those times your child understands why you are not responding: At some point you already hashed this out, you gave a reply, and your child knows where you stand. Plus, unless you are a very unhealthy parent, you will continue talking with your child about a number of other things. We must accept this form of parenting from our Father.

I and others have learned that when we feel blocked with something we desperately want to pursue with God or when it "seems" He is silent, we should try changing the subject or asking Him if this is something He is not going to address with us. Other times I may go to more familiar ground, maybe praise and thank Him or ask Him about what we are going to be doing today or working on together.

As I have learned to expect that God *wants* to communicate, I have indeed experienced conversation with Him as a typical and common way of life—a normal way of life for a Christian.

VALIDATING WE ARE HEARING GOD

When people first begin to open up to the idea that the Holy Spirit wants to communicate regularly with their spirits in a two-way conversation, their immediate questions generally have to do with, "But how can I tell it's *really* God?"

All of us have heard outlandish explanations of how "God" has led someone into foolish and sinful behavior. I have heard way too many times how people are certain God has brought a particular man or woman into their lives—even though they are already married. I've also heard people say they can really connect with God when they are high from drugs or alcohol. Or that God wanted them to cash in all their savings and retirement to support a certain Christian's vision.

I applaud the desire not to demean God by claiming such directives are from Him; I would never want to participate in this type of off-base "hearing." This is why I emphasize that we must hear God accurately and skillfully. We must have ways to validate the authenticity of what we are hearing.

The Authority of the Bible

The most obvious validation is that nothing we hear from God can ever contradict or compromise Scripture. We know this based upon the character of God. God cannot lie or change, and He is not the author of confusion. Always check out your understanding of what you think the Lord is saying to you based upon God's revealed truth in the Bible. In addition, it is important to know that God's revealed Word, the Bible, is complete. Nothing God communicates to His children will be new "revelation."

Here is a good way to picture this truth. Think of the breadth of knowledge we have about God as revealed through the Bible as a large circle, and the specific truths God shares with us through His Holy Spirit as a smaller circle within that larger circle. Nothing God reveals to us now will forge new doctrine or contradict what He has revealed through Scripture. All will be within the larger circle.

It is probable God will reveal something that is "new" to us, but this can still be confirmed by Scripture. He may also reveal something that may correct a mistaken understanding of Himself or of Scripture. But anything we think we hear from the Lord that is not inside the larger circle cannot be from God. He may give us direction on a situation, such as a parenting or ministry question, that is not *addressed* by Scripture. But even then, His input will be congruent with His character and will as revealed in Scripture.

Every aspect of communicating with God always has and always will fall under the authority of the written Word of God, the Bible. In no way at any time will a Christian hear words from God that contradict or compromise the written Word of God.

Experience Is Not the Yardstick

Another important point in discerning authenticity is never to judge truth by experience, like the person in an affair believing the other person is a gift from God because of how they can pray and study the Bible together. Or the person who feels that because a wonderful opportunity came along it must be from God. Never assume that an experience or circumstance that "feels" good to you is automatically from God. Satan is a master of deception.

Many solid believers are not prone to fall for these kinds of deceptions; most know better than to condone an affair or other obvious sin, or call an outlandish scheme God's will for them. Instead, oddly, they fall into a different error. They mistrust an experience when it is "too good." Somewhat surprisingly, many Christians doubt they have heard accurately from the Lord when He says something that makes them feel wonderful. They expect to hear God's correction and discipline and instructions on what they should be doing. Therefore when the Lord wishes to affirm them, it can seem suspect. Watch how Satan will attempt to "rob" you at times like these and tempt you to discard what you have heard. The same is often true when God attempts to lavish you with His love. For many, this is just too much; it seems almost impossible to believe, because their life and church experiences have convinced them this is not who God is. Yet our Father is known for His lavish and unconditional love.

My suggestion is that when we believe we have accurately heard from God (especially on anything of importance or involving a significant life change), we should ask mature Christians who have skill in hearing God to meet with the Lord over what we think we are hearing. When I do this I do not ask for the other persons' opinions. I show them my written conversation with God and ask them to meet with the Lord, discuss it with Him, and then share the results with me.

Even when we have validated what we are hearing, we must also pay attention to how we are *interpreting* it.

Hearing Accurately Doesn't Mean We Understand Correctly

After doing years of marriage counseling, I have learned it is entirely possible to hear accurately the words others are saying and yet completely misunderstand what they are communicating. Often, during a spirited marriage counseling session, I'll notice one person getting quite upset. I will stop and ask, "What do hear your spouse saying?" Many times people's answers are not close to what was just said. But sometimes they do accurately repeat what their spouses said, and while they are repeating it, they get even *more* upset. Confused, I ask why they are so upset. When they share what is going on, many times it is clear that although they heard the words accurately, they completely misunderstood.

For example, a wife may say, "I feel so unloved. All I really want is my husband." Husbands, especially if feeling defensive and helpless, often report, "She is saying I do not love her. I cannot believe this. Then when she says she wants me … goodness, what more do I have to do! I work hard—real hard—and come home every night. I don't go drinking or carousing. I just don't know. I am giving her all I have to give."

Notice the wife never said her husband does not love her; she simply says she "feels" unloved. And she did not say that her husband is not working hard or that he is out carousing. Do you see how sometimes we can hear words accurately but misunderstand their meaning? What the wife is saying is, "What would make me *feel* loved is connecting with him, communicating on a deep level emotionally and spiritually. I want to know him and what is really going on within him."

We can do something similar as we "interpret" the words we hear from God. The Lord may say to us during a discussion about a difficult job situation, "I have something special I want to give you because I value and cherish you." We may run with that and think God said He would give us the promotion we've been wanting. But is that what He said? He might have something very different in mind, such as giving us an experience of being loved and valued in the midst of a time of mistreatment or injustice, or He might want to give us a new avenue for rest and refreshment even though our job situation remains unchanged.

Hearing words and understanding them accurately are two different skills, whether you're hearing from God about a decision, about correction or discipline, about how He wants you to pray for someone, or even about words of affection and affirmation that you question and just cannot receive. To progress in these skills we must practice, and we must ensure accuracy while we practice. The best way to do this is to ask God about it. Write out what you have heard Him say and what you believe it to mean and then ask Him if your understanding is accurate. Then ask someone who has good skills in communicating with God to read your dialogue and your understanding of what you have heard. Ask him or her to meet with the Lord about your conversation with Him, listen to Him, and then report the results of that meeting.

Because validating that you are hearing accurately is so important, this is something I will be talking with you about more throughout this book. I'll help you understand what to look for and what to be aware of. And, at the end of the book, I'll even summarize what we have discussed. For now, though, simply be assured that discernment is important, and be willing to take the first steps to grow in it.

HUMILITY AND WILLINGNESS TO GROW ARE KEY

Discerning you are accurately hearing God is something you will gain skill in as you practice. Don't let the fact that you may be new to this type of discernment stop you from beginning to listen for what God deeply desires for you.

As with any new skill, whether playing a musical instrument or doing a new sport or using use an advanced technical device, there is a learning curve. How sad it would be if we were only willing to try developing a new skill if we have already some natural propensity. For most of us, learning a new skill is very humbling and stretching.

I will never forget my first effort at downhill snow skiing. Being an avid and advanced surfer, I "knew" skiing would be a piece of cake. But after spending a day on the simplest bunny slopes and failing miserably, I took off my skis and walked down the mountain. I remember mumbling to myself that there was no chance I would ever again subject myself to such a complete waste of time.

The main problem was, I was at the ski resort as the speaker at a singles conference; therefore, my skiing deficiencies could not be hidden. One of the singles at this conference would not accept my determination not to waste my time on something so frustrating and took it upon himself to coach me in this sport that he loved. After one of the evening sessions, he drilled me on the basics, and, much to my surprise, I learned that the most fundamental skill of skiing—keeping your weight forward at all times—was contrary to my surfing instincts. No wonder I'd failed so badly!

The next day he patiently gave up a day of advanced skiing with his friends to coach me. At the end of the day, I was hooked with the sport. I have loved skiing ever since. I am so grateful I didn't quit when I really wanted to. God has used this lesson as a reminder for me time and time again when I face something new and uncomfortable.

When you begin listening to God, may you be so bold as to develop new skills and go through the common pattern of starting at "I am just not good at this and I don't think I can learn this," to move to, "Well maybe I am not hopeless but I am sure making lots of mistakes" to, "I think I might be getting this" to, "I am so glad I did not quit; this is so worth the effort and frustration and sense of humiliation."

In learning how to communicate with God, most people will have these feelings, along with very little confidence in what they are doing—as well as feeling quite uncomfortable. For most, the start is awkward and seems artificial and mechanical. Plus, our first attempts will likely not be accurate. But the great news is that every single Christian of every age and culture and intellectual ability has a superb, personal coach: God the Holy Spirit. He loves to train every one of His own, and His patience and encouraging ways set Him apart as the ultimate coach.

Please do not allow unsettling feelings or your intellectual and analytical comfort zone to block you from what I consider the greatest gift God has given me since I accepted Jesus Christ as my Lord and Savior: the ability to communicate with Him.

As you get started conversing with God, I'd suggest reviewing what the Holy Spirit does for and in you (see chapter 4). You can trust Him to communicate in line with His fruit and with God's character. Jesus your Good Shepherd will lead and guard you. Your Father will superintend you, just like any Father helping His child learn to walk or talk. And, as a good Father, He will celebrate and rejoice over your first steps and first words!

Practice Session

Skills You're Acquiring and Practicing

- Being a "beginner" dialoguer who is learning
- Discerning God's "voice"
- Expecting God to communicate with you relationally

Your Assignment

This time, we are moving from a letter format to a dialogue format (though you may continue writing letters, if you wish). In a dialogue format, you say one thing to the Father, then pause and allow Him to respond to what you said.

Then you respond to what you heard from Him.

Continue to write down both what you are saying to Him and what He is saying to you.

Pointers

- *Expect uncertainty.* As you move into more of a dialogue format, you may feel a little intimidated. This is typical—and normal. Especially if you're new to listening to God, you can expect many of the uncertainties you would feel at beginning anything new.

- *Expect that God wants to speak with you.* "Who am I to think I am hearing from God," many people say. Well, you're His dearly loved child, and He has promised that His Holy Spirit will testify about that to your spirit (Romans 8:16).

- *Write now, discern later.* Go ahead and write down what you think you're hearing. If you tend toward analytical thinking, please set that aside for a bit (if you get too analytical, you can block yourself from hearing God). If you're not sure about it, just make a note and keep on going.

  That's the beauty of doing this in writing; you can come back later and ask God to help you discern what was really Him. God will help confirm what was of Him and what has parts of you mixed in. If you're like most people I've mentored, you'll discover that much of what you're hearing really is from Him.

- *Use a scene or picture.* Remember that it may be helpful to picture a setting for your conversation (see appendix D).

Sample Dialogue

I call this a dialogue because it uses a back-and-forth format to record a two-way conversation with God (God's responses are italic). When I say *dialogue* for the rest of the book, this is the format I'm talking about.

I've gathered the samples on these pages from people I've mentored over the years. You'll notice that each dialogue feels and sounds different because God is personal and speaks to people differently. The following dialogue is one of the first times Connie, my collaborator on this book, had a back-and-forth conversation with God, and she was still wrestling with the idea that God wanted a *real* relationship with her.

I've got so much to talk about, but I feel awkward being the one doing all the talking now that I know You want to talk with me. Is it okay if I just chatter on about anything and everything?

Yes, but don't expect Me to keep silent. I'm going to have things to say.

I've got questions—so many questions.

But ... I'm not necessarily here to give answers. This is about relationship. That's the point.

I know a whole lot about processing ideas and asking questions. I don't know much about relationship. That's a whole different grid for me. If this is a relationship, then I would treat it as one.

Good! Let Me out of your journal and into your life. I'm not simply for a morning devotional time. You're acting as if I'm a relationship you can check in with when you have the emotional capacity for it. Or like I'm away traveling and can only make a rare five-minute international call. I'm far, far closer than that. Far more intimate.

You know how much that scares me.

Yes, and I know the furies that rose up the last time we touched on it. "Father, Friend, Savior" ... you're going to experience Me in all these ways.

Scared, that's what I am. Scared. I *like* my Lone Ranger world. And You're striking at the very core of it.

Yes, I am, aren't I?

I could swear I heard a delighted chuckle there.

And why wouldn't I be delighted? Finally, finally, I get to have the relationship with you that I've longed for ... that I made you for. This door is finally open to Me.

I'm overwhelmed. I don't know how to respond. This is where I go sorta blank.

You've been praying for this, haven't you?

I've been praying for this? I've opened the door? How? Oh. I guess I have been praying that Ephesians prayer about "being established and rooted in love." Okay, yeah, I guess I have been praying for this.

Get ready. "I'm going to love you, like nobody's loved you, come rain or come shine." That's going to be our song, you know.

And what else does that song say?

Umm ... that *I'm* going to love you.

Follow-up Coaching

As you begin to dialogue with God, you may encounter some common blocks to hearing Him. I would like to talk about these blocks in some depth. Before you begin working through this coaching, read it over. Then come back and work through the sections that seem most applicable to you.

You don't need to work through everything here. Ask God, "Would You direct me to the area(s) where You want me to focus?" Also, you can come back later and complete any other sections that you may need.

Blocked by Lack of Experience and Awareness

1. In this area, you're blocked because you don't know what you're listening for, you don't know what to expect, and you don't have any experience sorting out what you're hearing.

Do you resonate with any of the following perceptions of the process of hearing from God?

a. "God's thoughts in my mind are going to sound special and 'huge.'"

b. "Most people who hear from God are naturals at it. I either get it or I don't."

c. "I'm going to have to work really hard to hear from God."

d. "When I try to hear from God, all I get is 'static' or random thoughts. Nothing ever happens."

e. "I sorta 'hear' something, but I'm just making this up. I can't trust myself to hear."

f. "I don't want to "claim" to hear God when really all I'm doing is opening myself up to lies, either from the enemy or my wishful thinking."

g. "This isn't for me because I just can't concentrate; I can't sit still. My mind goes all over the place."

The Reality. Did you identify with any of those perceptions? Here are the realities that counteract them, and some next steps you can take as you try another dialogue using these helps.

a. **Reality:** Most of the time, the "thoughts" from God that come into your mind are not going to sound booming or "huge." They will be somewhat like the thoughts you normally hear, but the tone and content will be God's.

   What to do: Don't filter out something that sounds like your thoughts. Instead, write it down and let God keep the conversation going.

b. **Reality:** While some people are more sensitive or perceptive than others, most people *aren't* naturals at hearing God. They have to learn how to acquire this skill and get better over time as they pay attention and practice.

   What to do: Practice "tuning in" to God's communication. Write down what you *think* He might say to you, using the two Luke 11 word pictures, without dismissing or over-analyzing because you're unsure. Gradually, you will gain confidence and the ability to discern.

c. **Reality:** Though you will have to put in some effort and practice as well as give God an opening to speak, you don't have to generate anything or make anything happen. You're entering into a real conversation with a real Person, a Father and Friend who *wants* to talk with You and ensure you hear Him. Actually, it is His responsibility to make this work.

   What to do: Tell God you think this will be hard work, and invite Him to reassure you or share some of His thoughts with you.

d. **Reality:** More is probably happening than you realize. Don't analyze it away. Sometimes what you label a "random" thought really *is* God. As you practice writing down what you seem to be hearing, you'll get better at separating God's thoughts from "background noise."

What to do: Risk writing down the thoughts that come into your mind. If you don't hear anything, go back to speculating: Reread what you shared and write down what you think God might say. Trust God to interrupt your thoughts. If a song, Scripture passage, picture, quote, or memory comes to mind, describe it briefly, and let God respond.

e./f. ***Reality:*** Mistrust can make many people "pre-discard" much of what God might be saying or not even try because of their fear. The truth is, God is not interested in having you claim your own thoughts as His, nor does He want you to be deceived. You are not in this alone! God wants to and will help you hear Him and discern His thoughts from yours.

What to do: Pray before you begin listening, asking God to help you hear only His voice, to protect the conversation from any interference and from deception. Then simply get started, trusting that as you draw near to God, He is also drawing near to you (James 4:8).

g. ***Reality:*** Distraction is common in any relationship (ask my wife!), but it is not a deal-breaker. Everyone faces it, particularly in our multi-tasking, high-performance world.

What to do: Be sure you're writing down your conversation. When you get distracted, just look back and pick up where you left off. If you need to, go to a place where you *can* sit still, such as a coffee shop, a public bench, or a library.

Blocked by Misconceptions or False Beliefs

2. As we have already talked about, false beliefs can also block us from hearing what God is saying. Here are some common misconceptions that might block you when you're trying to hear Him (for more infor-

mation, review "blocked by a misconception" in the coaching portion of chapter 2):

- "If I do hear from God, He's just going to scold me and tell me all the stuff I'm doing wrong."

- "There's too much wrong in my life for God to speak to me. I have to get myself right before I can expect Him to talk with me."

- "There's not much benefit for me in listening to God the way we're talking about. In fact, I'm not even sure I trust Him enough to want to hear from Him. We'll probably get along best if we're not too close."

a. Do any of those describe you? If so, which ones? Or did any other "blocking" thoughts come to you when you were listening for God? If so, what were they?

b. It breaks the power of these thoughts when we bring them out of the shadows and into the light. Write a few sentences telling God what you've been thinking and ask Him to help you believe truth about Him and how He wants to relate with you.

c. Now listen for His response to you (or speculate on it), and write it down.

Blocked by Enemy Interference

3. This block is very common because Satan doesn't want you in intimate connection with God—powerful things will happen in and through you when you are! So you can *expect* to encounter spiritual warfare as you begin to relate with God in the ways I am teaching you to in this course. The presence of spiritual warfare is actually

encouraging; there is something going on that is costly to the evil one and his plans.

This interference may take some of the following forms:

- Confusion, fogginess, and distraction when you begin listening for God.

- Seemingly unrelated life circumstances discourage you and keep you from being able to spend time with God or connect with Him.

- You feel "oppressed" and blocked, as if you're walking through thick mud; everything is harder and feels difficult to do.

- When you sit down to talk with God, you write a few words, hear yourself thinking, "I can't do this," "It's too hard," "I'll never get this," "This is stupid," "I shouldn't be doing this," "I'm just making this all up," or "This is just a total waste of time"—and you just quit and go do something else.

a. Have you experienced any of this so far in this course? If so, what?

b. If you sense any of this happening, take it to God and talk with Him about it openly; bringing these areas of confusion or oppression out of the darkness and into God's light helps release their hold over you. Listen to God share His perspective, His encouragement, and His commitment to you. When you see these oppressions for what they are, they lose a gigantic amount of power to affect you.

Tell God, "Lord, I think I may be experiencing oppression right now in the form of _____. Is this Satan's attempt to mess me up? Please help me with this." Make notes of your conversation.

In addition:

- As you begin a dialogue, tell God you know He wants you to hear Him, and ask Him to help you hear only His Holy Spirit, blocking out all other influences or voices.

- Begin to work with God to relinquish any longstanding lies or grudges you are holding against Him, as well as any areas of sin, unforgiveness, bitterness, hardness, or numbness that have taken hold in your life. These are all areas that block you from God and make you susceptible to His enemy. These changes generally won't happen overnight, but your Father wants you to have freedom and will lead you toward that freedom as you talk and relate with Him. I love what God says in Isaiah 43: "I, even I, am He who blots out your transgressions for my own sake, and remembers your sins no more" (verse 25).

Blocked by Lifestyle Distractions

4. Hearing God and discerning His voice isn't a skill that comes automatically. You need to be intentional about it, which means investing some time and attention. To put it bluntly: You won't hear from God if you never get quiet enough to let Him speak. God will not shout to be heard over the distractions in your life.

"But I have this gut-wrenching situation going on ..." you might be saying. And it's true; our lives are filled with relationships and responsibilities and stress. You might be a mom with young kids. You might be working twelve hours a day in a noise-filled job. You might be chronically ill or caring for elderly parents ... or all of the above. Trust me: There is a way for you to converse with God in the middle of it. I have never yet met a person who *wanted* to hear God but wasn't able to because of a life situation. I absolutely trust that God has a customized solution for you. Why don't you ask Him about it, using one of these prompts:

- "Father, I can't see how this 'talking with You' thing is going to happen. But I have five minutes right now. Please show me how to make this work."

- "Good Friend, I'm starving for friendship, but I don't have time for it. What can we do?"

- "Father, if I talk to You right now, I will not have time to _____. Would You be willing to somehow make this work out if I first talk to You?"

I have come to God like this again and again and again, and, miraculously (to me), He always makes it work out. I have had times when I get called to do a last-minute speaking engagement, and I only have two hours to prepare—and yet it takes a minimum of six hours preparation to do justice to the opportunity. It seems like the best I can do is going to be barely adequate.

What I have done is to take as much time as necessary to share my dilemma with the Lord, tell Him it feels ("terrifying"), and allow Him to minister to me, comfort me, and encourage me. Then we begin working on the speaking assignment. Some of the best presentations I have ever done have resulted from trusting God in this fashion and going against every fiber of reason within me.

Now, if stress and responsibilities are blocking you from talking with Him, share these thoughts with the Lord and write down what He says to you.

Blocked by an Inability to Relate Fully with God.

5. When we are shut down in certain areas of relationship with God, we block our ability to hear Him in those areas. As we've already seen, sometimes those shut-down areas come from misconceptions about God. But sometimes the following areas can block His voice as well.

- *General inability to relate.* If we're not used to giving and receiving affection with people, it will be hard to hear affection from God.

- *A factual approach to life.* Because all of us are created in God's image and God is an emotional God, every one of us has emotions. However, many of us live as if we do not have any. This will cause us to look to God for information and facts, but won't allow us to hear Him in other areas, especially in areas that are dominated by our emotions, whether we are in touch with them or not.

- *Narrow expectations / "God in a box."* Our theology, upbringing, and life experiences all form what we expect from God. If we don't think He cares about "silly" things, we won't hear Him if He tries to joke with us. If we don't expect Him to initiate with us personally, we won't notice when He tries to say something to us during a business meeting.

- *Unhealed heart wounds.* Circumstances and events in our past can leave us numb or scarred, blocking our ability to relate with other people—or God. A common example is an abusive father; the scarring from what he did can render us seemingly incapable of relating with God as Father; others may have experienced devastating physical or sexual abuse.

a. Do you recognize yourself in any of these areas? If so, which one(s)?

b. Talk with God about it. Tell Him what you're sensing, and how you feel that might affect your ability to talk with Him. Ask Him for His input. Make notes of your conversation.

These areas where you may be shut down or blocked will likely not disappear overnight; that's fine! You're in a long-term relationship with God, and you can trust that He *will* bring to completion the plans He has started in you. Just take the next step in relating with Him—and keep going with this course. The next chapters will teach you a great deal about relationships and will help address some of these areas.

Intimacy through Sharing and Receiving

The first part of this book laid the foundation for relational, two-way communication with God and described what that conversation is like. In your assignments, you practiced writing letters and dialogues with God and took first steps to discern His voice. For the rest of the course, I will ask you to continue writing these two-way dialogues with God. This is the core "method" we will use to communicate with Him.

In these next few chapters, I want to turn our attention to some practical skills that will advance your ability to communicate relationally with God. But first, let me ask you a question:

When you think about God's love for you, which of these three options most accurately describes you?

a. I think God loves me.

b. I *know* God loves me.

c. I *feel* loved by God on a regular basis.

INTIMACY WITH GOD

When I have asked others this question, virtually all Christians will say they *think* it's true that God loves them. They have read verses that tell them God is love, and they know John 3:16 about God's love for the world. God's love is one of the first things they were taught about Him.

A smaller group says, "I really *know* God loves me in a way that is beyond just thinking He loves me." This group is certain of their belief in God's love and knows that love is personal for them.

When people choose to be completely honest (and not just say what they think they should say or what they would like to be able to say) very few claim the third option: "I regularly *feel* loved by God." Many say, "There are times I feel loved by God, especially when He blesses me so obviously I know it's Him. But to say I feel loved by God in the way I feel loved by my mom or dad or spouse or friends? No, I don't *feel* loved like that."

If someone would have asked me that question years ago—even when I was in seminary—I would have chosen option b, "I know God loves me," because I knew that's what the Bible said. It wouldn't have occurred to me question whether I was experiencing being loved. In fact, the question wouldn't even have computed. Like the vast majority of men, that way of thinking was foreign. I wasn't experiencing God's love, didn't feel any need to experience it, and didn't think about it. However, also like most men, I had a strong, real need to be deeply loved; I just had zero *felt* need for it.

In addition, if someone had asked about my love for God, citing God's command to love Him with all my heart, soul, mind, and strength, I probably would have said that command meant I should love God "a lot," but I would have had a hard time explaining what loving Him was like without going into what I did for Him, such as participating in church and doing Bible study and serving Him. I just did not understand the relational love that the Father wants with each of His kids.

That I and others would give these responses grieves me. The loving connection our Father desires with us is truly beyond our full understanding. John talks about this love in 1 John 4: "This is love: not that we loved God, but that he loved us and sent his Son as an atoning sacrifice for our sins" (v. 10). God's request for our love in response to His is equally astounding: "You shall love the Lord your God with all your heart, and with all your soul, and with all your mind," (Matthew 22:37, NASB). Most of us would like to be able to follow this command.

I think the issue lies with us, not the ways in which our Father loves us. The largest part of the problem is that we do not know how to communicate relationally with God as Luke 11 teaches. It is not that we don't want to be close to God; most of us just do not know how. In order to relate with God at the level He desires, we must learn how to enter into intimacy with Him.

Intimacy is an intriguing word. Men shudder at it and immediately become uncomfortable—even defensive—when they hear it. Most of us men fear intimacy and don't like to talk about it. Most women, on the other hand, yearn for intimacy, dream about it, and will do astounding things in search of it. Yet most of them seem disappointed by the lack of it. So bringing up "intimacy" means raising an awkward concept for both men and women. Yet intimacy is at the core of communicating with God. If I could pick only one word to describe what God wants with His kids, I'd pick *intimacy*. If you have intimacy you have love.

Quite simply, *intimacy happens when two people share the innermost part of themselves and each receives what the other shares.* Let's look at these two aspects of intimate communication: vulnerable sharing and receiving.

VULNERABLY SHARING OUR TRUE SELVES

The first aspect of intimacy is sharing the innermost part of ourselves with another person. The two most important components here are *vulnerability* and *trust*. We cannot experience intimacy unless we become vulnerable with a friend, partner, or family member, and we cannot be vulnerable without trust. Now, to most men—and many women—*vulnerability* is a word much like *intimacy*. Men especially do not like vulnerability and avoid it like the plague. Being vulnerable means feeling exposed; it is uncomfortable. When we are vulnerable, what people think of us and how they respond to us is huge. This is why we can only do it with someone we deeply trust.

Being vulnerable requires disclosing the deeper, emotional parts of ourselves. This isn't something most of us do naturally—we tend to stay on the surface. I have little problem sharing my thoughts and opinions with others. If I'm standing in a group of strangers and someone brings up something I find interesting, I can share my thoughts without any difficulty. The same is true of strong opinions, such as whether the Cowboys can win a championship with our present coach or how the United States should help other countries after a natural disaster.

Sharing myself at this level is not hard for me or for most people. What is hard—what very few men are willing to do—is to be open about my feelings. That crosses the line into vulnerability. Now, we all have some emotions we are comfortable expressing. Most people are fine if others see they are happy. Many people also easily display irritation, anger, or passion for ideas or causes. But to be vulnerable about emotions that make us feel exposed and powerless? We'd rather not do that.

I recently had a heart test after having some chest pains. Because I don't like to display vulnerability, when people asked, "How are you feeling about the test?" I'd say, "I'm doing okay. I feel fine now, the test seemed to go all right, and I'm waiting for the results."

But how would it sound if I chose to be vulnerable and put words to my feelings, something I only do with a few people with whom I'm intimate and trust fully? I would have said, "I am feeling out of control, vulnerable, and apprehensive. I know the Lord is with me and watching over me, but this is hard."

Consider what vulnerability sounds like in some other situations:

- "I understand you were laid off. How are you doing?"
  Typical: "Well, it's not what I'd choose, but I'm sure I'll manage somehow."
  Vulnerable: "I'm feeling lost, confused, and helpless. I'm not sure what we are going to do."

- "I understand your daughter-in-law lost the baby. How are you doing?"
  Typical: "It's a really tough time for her. The doctor says she'll be okay and they can try again."
  Vulnerable: "I am devastated. I am not good at this kind of grief. I wish I knew what to say to comfort them. I feel so powerless."

Can you see the difference between the vulnerable answers and the ones we would normally give? Because we're not accustomed to vulnerability in our human relationships, it also doesn't occur to us to be vulnerable with God. This is particularly true if we've only been taught to see Him as our King and Master. Or if we think He's just going to tell us to be joyful and content about whatever our burden is. Our same habits of self-protection are firmly in place when we pray, and they keep us from experiencing the love and care of our perfect Parent.

David, who God says was a man after His own heart, is my favorite biblical character. David was also a mighty warrior, truly a "man's" man. When I first began to see David's vulnerability with the Lord, I was blown away. Listen to him openly share his emotions: "Be merciful to me, O Lord, for I am in distress; my eyes grow weak with sorrow, my soul and my body with grief. My life is consumed by anguish and my years by groaning; my strength fails because of my affliction, and my bones grow weak" (Psalm 31:9-10).

Many people have found it helpful to pray David's psalms just for this reason: They help us express things we have difficulty identifying, much less talking about.

Fortunately the most trustworthy person we will ever encounter is the Lord God. He not only invites you, He *commands* you to cast "all your cares upon Him, for He cares for you" (1 Peter 5:7, NKJV). The Lord wants us; He wants oneness with us. He wants us to experience unparalleled intimacy with Him—great trust along with great vulnerability. We simply cannot do this by only telling Him about our thoughts and requests. We must trust Him with our emotions and talk about the innermost parts of who we are.

Recently I talked with God about some hurtful words someone was speaking about me behind my back. I didn't want to admit this was really getting to me because I wanted to tough it out. But I did tell God I was hurt and embarrassed and very angry.

My Father and Friend gave me great understanding and care. Then He told me some of the reasons this was bothering me so much, and He exposed some past pain that these present words were "pricking." He said He wanted to bring healing to these old wounds so they would not be so easily reopened. He even told me He "allowed" this present pain so I would be open to hearing what He wished to do with me. I was blown away. I don't think I would ever have seen this, and I certainly would not have received this help from my faithful Friend unless I'd been willing to be vulnerable and tell Him how I was feeling.

As we choose to enter into intimacy by vulnerably trusting God with our feelings, what He gives us in return comprises much of the best part of being His son or daughter or friend while we are still here on earth. To feel unconditionally loved, to feel valued and treasured, to feel protected and accepted and cared for—goodness, what is better than this?

RECEIVING WHAT GOD WANTS TO GIVE US

But we won't fully feel that unless we learn the next aspect of intimacy with God: *receiving* what He wants to give us. Just as God took in what we were saying and responded to us when we vulnerably shared ourselves, we need to take in what *He* wants to say to us and respond to Him. Most of us have a deficit here because we simply haven't been taught how to do it.

To *receive* means to take hold of something or to take it into our possession and own it. Relationally, receiving means to take from another by hearing and allow what we are hearing to *touch* us. When we receive something someone tells us, we allow it to sink in. We notice what we are feeling and share our feelings with the other person (this is where we again risk some vulnerability).

Here are some examples of what our typical responses sound like, and what it would sound like to *receive* what is being said to us:

* "You sure look nice."
  Typical. "Isn't it amazing how good clothes can make almost anyone look presentable?"
  Receiving. "Thank you so much. I was feeling somewhat insecure about this outfit. I feel reassured by you noticing."

* "Thanks for helping me with this project. I don't know how I could have done it without you."
  Typical. "It was nothing. At best I just saved you a few minutes."
  Receiving. "Hearing you say that means very much to me. You're important to me and I wanted you to know that."

* "You are such a good friend; I appreciate you."
  Typical. "Let me tell you who is a good friend. Now, Sally is really a good friend."

Receiving. "Thank you, I feel appreciated. I'm so grateful I have a friend like you who is so encouraging."

• "You are so smart. What an excellent way to explain that difficulty."
Typical. "You should have seen me yesterday, lost as a goose trying to get to Central Market."
Receiving. "I appreciate your affirmation. I'm not very good at receiving; it makes me uncomfortable. It's good for me to hear that what I said was helpful."

Receiving is a wonderful way of connecting with someone we care about and fostering closeness and intimacy. And receiving is a key skill that will enable us to enter into the loving relationship with God that He so desires to share with us. He wants to give us *Himself,* and love us, care for us, and minister to us. When we don't receive from Him, we are brushing Him off and deflecting the relationship.

Many of us have experienced wanting to give a blessing to our children, to tell them how deeply we love them or admire them or are proud of them. Yet when we say something it just rolls off them. I can remember a time when I told my teen daughter how much I loved her and how wonderful she was only to have her respond, "You have to say that; you're my father." No matter how hard I tried to explain or give evidence of what I knew to be true, she wouldn't take it in or let it affect and touch her. She wouldn't *receive* it from me. For a dad who deeply loves his daughter not to be able to encourage her or minister to her—well, it was distressing and painful.

Just as we are saddened and hurt when others won't receive from us and let our care affect them, God is affected by our refusal of the relationship and care He offers. Jesus lamented, "O Jerusalem, Jerusalem … how often I have longed to gather your children together, as a hen gathers her chicks under her wings, but you were not willing"

(Matthew 23:37). So often we, too, deflect God's desire to gather us under His wings.

He might say, "My child, I love the way you helped Terry and really inconvenienced yourself and did it out of joy. That pleased me greatly and I want you to know how proud I am of you." That's an amazing thing to hear! Yet we deflect it by responding, "Why wouldn't I have done that? I want to serve You." Receiving it would mean saying something like this: "Father, hearing You say that makes me feel wonderful—affirmed, encouraged, and honored."

In the following dialogue, notice how well my friend does at telling God how she is feeling, taking in what He shares with her, letting it affect her, and then responding back to Him.

Good morning, Father.

Good morning daughter. Please share with Me how you are feeling.

Oh, Father, you know I feel so tired and weak right now. I am struggling with feeling like I have failed and that You are distant. Would You show me what is true?

Sweet girl, I love you so. I love that you want to come and talk with Me. You trust Me and see your need of Me. I feel such affection and protection for you. My daughter has come. I am here. I am with you.

My child, the enemy does want to exhaust and discourage you. He desires to slow down My work and shut you down. He desires to put out your passion. I am using you today and I will give you the words to speak. My strength is made perfect in your weakness. My power over sin and death is stronger than anything that will come against you today. Nothing and no one can separate you from My love and My power. All that I am is yours for the asking. I give to you now all that you will need today.

Oh, Father. I feel such rest in your presence. I feel understood and so cared for. I give you everything that weighs on me. Thank you for Jesus. Thank you for the victory that is mine because of the victory that IS His. The prince of darkness cannot harm me. I am in my Father's hand. I love You. Lord, You are everything I need. I wish I could stay alone with You all day.

I know. You need rest. Thank you for all that you have done this week for your church family and for your family. The work of a mom is precious to Me, Lisa. You have loved your children and cared for them well this week. I see things that you do not. The way that you sat with Brandon, Mark, and Rachel and stopped all you felt you needed to do just to be with them. You and Rachel have had some wonderful talks. You are seeing her grow up and change and are so connected to her. It brings a smile to My face to see your love for your children.

Thank You, Father; thanks for how You affirm me. I do love them so. I am feeling like there is not enough of me to go around and yet You have shown me You are seeing my time with them. Please continue to help me with the balance of ministry, family, health, financial prudence, etc., … I so need to walk with You. I am overwhelmed.

I know. You have been sick and are physically tired. This has been a hard week for you, Lisa. I do want you to rest this week. I do want you to schedule a work time for you, K and B. They will share in this with you and come alongside you.

God does not do halfway, surface relationships with little emotional connection. True relationships with Him are full of deep love, and communication is the vehicle by which we experience that love. We cannot enter into genuine relational communication with God without entering into intimacy with Him. Intimacy is established when we trust God enough to vulnerably share our emotions with Him and when we receive what He wishes to give us.

Vulnerably sharing ourselves is a skill anyone can learn. Vulnerability with a God who is trustworthy opens up a depth in relationship that all desire but few attain. And when we learn how to receive God's care and affection and devotion to us, well, my experience is that this is the most loved and valued I have ever felt. I experience intimacy in the best sense of the word.

Practice Session

Skills You're Acquiring and Practicing

- Receiving from God
- Taking in God's affection
- Engaging in back-and-forth dialogue

Your Assignment

Please try another dialogue. This time, talk with God about an area of concern or fear. Consider sharing something about yourself that you don't feel good about. Tell the Father you are trying to be vulnerable with Him because you do trust Him and you want to get better at relating with Him. Use emotion words to tell Him what you're feeling.

Because we're often not good at naming our emotions, I've put a list of emotions in appendix C. Please use this list to help you put words to your feelings.

Pointers

- *Share feelings.* Use emotion words to tell God how you feel (use the list in appendix C to help you identify emotions). Even though it may feel awkward or even mechanical, use sentences such as,

  - "Father, I feel _____ when I think about this."

  - "I don't want to face this because it makes me feel _____."

  - "I wish I felt peace and contentment (and I've been beating myself up for not being able to get there), but instead I feel _____."

- *Practice receiving.* Try to take in what the Lord is saying to you, allow it to affect you emotionally, then tell Him how it affected you. Here are some sentences that will help you practice receiving (use the emotions list to help you fill in the blanks).

  - "When I hear You say this to me, I feel _____."

  - "Father, hearing You say these things is not easy for me. But I want to take them in and *really* believe them. I tend to think that when I'm able to receive, I will probably feel _____. Thanks for sharing this with me."

  - "I would like to be able to receive this and let it affect me. But honestly, right now all I'm feeling is _____." (Risk telling God what is really going on, even if you have to fill in the blank with "numb," "distant," "doubting," "scared" "apathetic," or some other emotion that feels bad or wrong to you. Your Father *wants* you to come to Him as you are, no matter wrong you feel you are.)

- *Anticipate God's feelings*: how He is feeling about you, how He is feeling about you working through this book, how He is feeling about what you are sharing with Him. Because He *is* love, don't be surprised if what He shares is very loving and affirming.

- *Expect to hear.* Take the risk of really hearing from God, even if you're not sure it's *actually* Him. Don't analyze away what you sense Him saying. It's okay to say, "God, I'm unsure this is really You, but I want to continue to practice hearing from You. Will You help me hear You ever more clearly and accurately?" Then continue the conversation.

Follow-up Coaching

As I continue to coach you, remember that my goal is not that you measure up to a standard or conform to a certain mold. Your relationship with God will be unique, and you will grow in it over time. In this coaching session, we will focus on the relationship skills discussed in this chapter.

1. Telling God your emotions. Did you use emotion words to tell God how you were feeling? Go back and underline them in your dialogue. If you're having a hard time finding emotion words in your dialogue, look at the feelings list in appendix C to identify ones that fit. Either go back to your dialogue and insert them or use the following sentence to tell God about them and then let Him respond to you: "Father, I need to follow up with what we were talking about. I'm feeling _____ about the situation … " Write down how God responds to you.

Principle to remember: Vulnerably sharing your emotions with God lets Him relate deeply with you, befriend you, and parent you in the ways He desires. It moves a conversation out of information mode and into relationship mode.

2. Receiving. Did God share His affection and love and care with you? If so, how did you do at receiving it? If you struggled, please try again. Choose one of the practice sentences below and fill in the blanks with emotion words (use the feeling-words list if you need help).

- "When I hear You say this to me, I feel _____."

- "Father, hearing You say these things is not easy for me. But I want to take them in and *really* believe them. I tend to think that when I'm able to receive, I will probably feel _____. Thanks for sharing this with me."

- "I would like to be able to receive this and let it affect me. But honestly, right now all I'm feeling is _____."

Principle to remember: Receiving what God is saying and letting it affect you is a pathway to developing genuine relationship as well as "ears to hear."

3. Being open about "ugly" or "messy" emotions. If you're feeling something negative, it can be tough to be open and honest about where you are—without putting a "Christian gloss" on it. For example, let's say you're upset with your spouse. Consider the difference in the following two ways of talking about it:

> *Typical.* "God, I'm upset. I know I'm supposed to love her. Will You give me patience?"
>
> *Vulnerable.* "God, I'm feeling hurt, misunderstood, and disregarded. And I feel guilty saying that because I know You want me to love her."

The second example names specific emotions and allows God to relate with you as you really are. Also, in the first, typical, way of praying, you are assuming the solution by telling God what you need (more patience). When you simply share vulnerably, you leave the door open for God to parent you as only He can. Maybe He'll reassure you that feeling hurt and disregarded doesn't mean you're not loving. Maybe He'll talk with you about your unreasonable expectations that fueled your hurt. Maybe He'll let you know that how your spouse treated you *is* hurtful. Maybe He'll talk about the guilt and pressure you feel about trying to live up to His standards.

In your dialogue, were you able to share negative emotions with God? Perhaps one of the following ways of answering this question resonates with you:

- "Sharing negative emotions is not a problem for me. I do it easily."

- "I do okay with conveying irritation or anger. I don't share hurt or vulnerability very well."

- "I don't have much tolerance for negative and messy emotions. It doesn't do any good to dredge things up. The point is just to get on with life."

- "I'd rather not go there; I don't want to be controlled by emotion."

- "I'm pretty even-keel. I don't really get upset about stuff."

The truth is, we all feel emotions of varying levels, whether we acknowledge them or not. If you were feeling bad but didn't know how to express it or didn't want to, take the risk of revisiting the dialogue, telling God what you were feeling (use the emotions list) and letting

Him respond to you. This is how you will grow relationally with Him. Write down what He tells you.

Principle to remember: God can handle mess. He actually does great with messes. Talk about the emotions you're actually feeling, whether they're positive, negative, or mixed. Just like God wants you to relate with Him as He truly is, He wants to relate with you as you truly are.

GAINING GOD'S PERSPECTIVE

I have thought about and meditated on and studied one of God's declarations for quite some time. I've concluded it is of utmost importance that we deeply understand this profound truth as we communicate with Him:

> "For My thoughts are not your thoughts, neither are your ways My ways," declares the LORD. "For as the heavens are higher than the earth, so are My ways higher than your ways, and My thoughts than your thoughts." (Isaiah 55:8-9, NASB)

God is telling us something here that is *always* true: His thoughts and ways are never our thoughts or ways. They will always be far superior to ours.

If God's thoughts and ways are not mine and are always infinitely superior, then why not continually trade mine for His? Why in the world would I want to live with inferior thoughts and ways when I have access to His 100 percent accurate thoughts and 100 percent perfect ways? I don't. I always want to exchange my limited perspective for His higher perspective.

For many years, I practiced getting God's thoughts on a situation by briefly writing out my view on something that was troubling me and then asking God for His perspective. After doing this countless times, I discovered I never once had the same perspective as God! I would think I had the best way to understand and address something, but after listening to the Lord share His thoughts, His viewpoint was always much more impressive and clearly more accurate than mine.

In the previous chapter, we looked at some relationship skills that help us develop intimacy with God. Now I want to talk about another core skill we need to develop if we are to communicate *with* our sovereign God: gaining His perspective. When we learn to hear His view of our situations, we can trade our perspectives for His. Living in God's perspective of what is going on in our lives enables us to live in truth and experience great freedom. In fact, this skill is so important that if you only get this one thing from the course, it will have been worth your time and investment.

A GOD'S-EYE VIEW

Let's look at some examples. Say someone is hateful to us, greatly offending and hurting us. Our perspective may be, "This is a mean, inconsiderate person whom I don't want to have anything to do with." We ask God for His perspective and suppose He shares with us that here is a person whose spouse has been unfaithful and who is going through a painful divorce. Would this make a difference in what we think and feel and how we might respond?

Or we have a child who is clearly in a state of rebellion. We tend to see it as a battle of wills and we, the parents, are going to win. We ask God for His perspective, and what if He reveals here is a child who is really hurting and is dealing with the pain in a very inappropriate way? Would this change how we will interact with our child?

Or we lose an important account at work because of the economy. We see this as bad luck that is going to reflect poorly on our job performance and we feel powerless to do anything about it. We ask God for His perspective and He says this is an opportunity to put into practice the passage in James 1 about counting a trial as a joy and learning to develop patience and perseverance. Does this affect how we feel and respond?

Or maybe we have always been closed off and reluctant to reveal who we really are. We share something vulnerable in a group that reveals creativity and unseen depth; later we reflect on what we've done and feel exposed, insecure, and foolish. We ask God for His perspective and He says He is ecstatic and rejoicing that who He made us to be had a chance to be seen and received by others. Would this diminish the grip of these feelings on us?

Or we are feeling insecure and somewhat fearful about the kids our teen son has been spending time with. We see this as a good time to pull in the reins and reinforce rules. We ask for God's perspective and He says this is a great relationship opportunity; this a good time to listen to our son talk about his friends and the concerns *he* has for them. Would having this perspective change how we deal with our teen?

In all these examples, adopting God's perspective greatly changes our experience of a situation, whether the situation itself changes or not.

TRANSFORMED THINKING

In order to gain God's perspective we must develop an awareness that we *have* perspectives and that they are *guaranteed* to be flawed.

Quite simply, a perspective is the way we see something. It is our assessment or interpretation, based on how we pull together and make sense of all the parts. We look at all the pieces, add them up, and come to a conclusion. For example, we look at a day that includes a flat tire, a missed meeting, an upset spouse, and overdue bills, and we label it "Lousy Day When I Could Do Nothing Right." This conclusion may be based on many things, including our long-term habits of thinking, our prejudices, our beliefs, our personality traits, our fears, our strengths, and our weaknesses.

When we live out of our perspectives, we are leaning on our own understanding (see Proverbs 3:5-6). Our faulty perspectives are guaranteed to generate all kinds of painful emotions. Our perspectives, especially when we are unsettled, tend to keep us in turmoil and enable Satan to have his way with us. In fact, when we're feeling at our worst, we need to know that's when our viewpoints are absolutely not to be trusted—even though that tends to be when we're the most convinced we know what the problem is. There is always a much more accurate way of looking at our situations, and we don't have access to it within ourselves; we need to ask God for His perspective.

God's perspective is what He sees. God wants us to understand that seeing what He sees is as important as doing what He wants. "I want to bring my light into this area of darkness for you," He is saying to us. "I want to bring you out of your inaccurate viewpoint and out of deception and into My light so you see what I see—then we'll talk about what you need to do." This is God parenting you by giving you His accurate understanding of what the event is all about. It is customized to you, and will often astound or amaze you. When we get God's perspective, we are liberated. We have His truth, and His truth sets us free from the powerful emotions generated by our viewpoints. We are also freed from Satan's ability to mess with us.

Listen to the Lord's appeal for us from Romans 12:2: "Let God transform you into a new person by changing the *way you think*. Then you will learn to know God's will for you, which is good and pleasing and perfect" (NLT, emphasis added). In essence God is saying, "I need to remake your approach to Me, to life, to yourself, to your family, to how you live with Me. Your way is based on a whole lot of self-trust, self-assessment, and self-determination. My way is based on truth and righteousness."

So how do we trade our perspective for God's?

PERSPECTIVE PRACTICE

We begin by putting our perspective into words. If we don't know our perspective, gaining God's doesn't have much impact because it's not correcting anything specific. If we don't see a problem, then receiving the antidote doesn't offer much help.

To put your perspective into words, ask yourself what your interpretation of the event or situation is. This helps you move past describing the events to giving your viewpoint of them. Describing them might sound like, "I can't believe all the work they are piling on me. I'm exhausted by working these hours and I have no time for a life." But your perspective or viewpoint might be, "I will not fail; I must succeed at any cost."

I have a friend who caused a minor fender bender; in the aftermath, she felt "bad" and "horrible." When she considered how she was adding up all the pieces, she realized she had concluded, "I have caused a problem that can never be set right. I'm not allowed to cause problems." Do you think this is the perspective of her loving and perfect Heavenly Father about this incident?

Sometimes you won't know what your perspective is; you'll just know you feel bad or tired or angry. When this happens, ask God to reveal what you are thinking that is making you feel so bad: "God, would You help me see what my view is of this 'mess'?"

After you have stated your perspective, tell God, "God, I really need your perspective right now. What is your view of this?" You want to make sure you listen for God's customized perspective for you, rather than asking yourself, "What does God want me to do?" and then answering, "Oh, I know. God would tell me, 'Trust me, be anxious for nothing.'" That type of statement is never a perspective. That's a directive. What's more, it's a directive that comes from your understanding and perspective of what is happening. God's perspective will be lovingly customized you.

This doesn't mean God's perspectives will always *feel* good or be what we might consider "positive." For example, I may be having an argument with my wife and tell God how insensitive Letty is being. His perspective may be that the problem is me and my defensiveness or the manner in which I am communicating. This will not feel good. I've been exposed, corrected, and convicted. But it is definitely good for me.

At other times, we're sobered because His perspective isn't the good news we'd hoped for. If He tells me, "Son, this is an opportunity for you to suffer as My Son suffered," I'm not going to be excited or feel warmed or affirmed. But I will expect that He has more to say and that He will also want to parent and befriend me. I may also hear, "Son, I know this is hard for you. And it's not fun for Me either. But you know this is part of the process, and didn't I do this with My own Son?" There will be a lot of compassion, understanding, direction, support, comfort, and encouragement. God's perspective may be sobering, but it will come with grace and mercy.

When God shares His perspective, our situations likely won't have changed, but because we can now view them accurately, how we experience them changes. Consider 2 Corinthians 12 where the apostle Paul recounts the dialogue he had with God, begging God to take away his "thorn in the flesh." Paul's perspective may have been that this was a painful handicap that sabotaged his ministry. God's perspective was that this was a painful handicap that allowed Paul to discover a profound truth and live in unbelievable freedom. God told him, "My grace is sufficient for you, for my power is made perfect in weakness" (verse 9). After that, Paul no longer asked God to take the thorn away. Instead, he was—amazingly—able to *boast* about his weakness because now he understood that the more weak he was, the more brilliantly God's power would be displayed.

When God gives His perspective, we must follow Paul's example and adopt it, keeping in mind that on issues of great pain, there is a good chance we will need to wrestle with God in order to gain and accept His perspective as our own. (We'll talk about wresting in the next chapter.) God's perspective on my friend's auto accident was that this was an opportunity for her to experience what it was like to be perfectly loved in the middle of a self-caused mess. My friend then had a choice: She could adopt God's view or stick with her own. This seems like a no-brainer, yet my friend told me she had to struggle to accept His gracious offer of love at a time when she didn't feel she deserved it.

Of course, you *can* choose to stick with your perspective. Can I encourage you, if you want to do that, to go ahead and be upfront about it? Tell God, "I don't want to offend You, but I think my perspective on this one is more accurate. Therefore I need to go with what I see and understand." Just admit that to your loving Father and best Friend, and see if you can really be so bold (not to mention miserable—remember that our viewpoints tend to keep us trapped; God's perspective always brings light and life).

TRANSFORMED PERSPECTIVES, TRANSFORMED LIVES

Try to imagine what would happen with our families, work problems, and worries if we corrected our perspectives on what we think is going on and then listened to what our Father wants us to do. Gaining God's perspective is such a practical skill that if I could convince you to start doing it every day, your life would be markedly different.

Take parenting. It would become much simpler if parents really learned to distrust their perspectives and knew how to come to God and listen to Him share His perspective (His "diagnosis," so to speak, of what is going on with each child), and then listen to what He would like Mom and Dad to do about it. Goodness—parenting skills could blossom beyond all we could think or even imagine!

As a counselor, learning to give up my viewpoint for God's has been invaluable. I have had an excellent education, great training, and more than thirty years of experience. Most people I counsel simply want to get my perspective on their problems and take advantage of my experience. Yet I would never give them what I consider to be such inferior treatment. Instead of me assessing their problem, I always ask God for His perspective. He is incredible at diagnosing a person's true root problem! I might think the person in front of me is about as selfish, self-centered, and spoiled as they come, but God tells me I'm dealing with someone who is severely damaged, abused, and relationally handicapped.

Here's a sample of a conversation where God shared His perspective about a difficult relationship:

Good morning, my Father.
Good morning My son.
Father, I must talk to You about Jim. I can't believe he's doing this. It's one thing to be aggravated, but it is quite another to withdraw and drop his responsibilities. Can't he see how wrong that is? And what about the people who are depending on him and looking up to him? I feel distrusted, and I feel disappointed, hurt, and dumped on. I wish I could just withdraw (like he has), but someone has to keep things going.
Son, I can see you are very upset—and rightfully so. What Jim is doing is not what I want, and others will be harmed by how he is dealing with his feelings. I see there is so much you want to do and say right now. I know you can't stand doing nothing when things are out of control.
Father, You do understand me and how I am feeling, and You know my tendencies. I don't want to cause a further mess and yet I can't imagine not doing something. I suspect my perspective is a bit different from Yours right now. Lord, what is Your perspective?

Jim is reacting to this conflict in typical ways for him. He is feeling insecure and inadequate. He is not good with conflict or comfortable with it; this is why he is withdrawing.

Okay, Father, that makes sense. I'm sorry he feels that way, but still—he's an adult and this isn't an adult way to deal with problems.

My son, I am not disagreeing with you, but this is Jim and this is what is going on. So the question now is how you are going to respond. And by the way, someone here—either you or Jim—is going to influence the other.

Lord, I know this is probably true, but I don't like it. Obviously now that You've given me Your perspective and put it out there that one of us will influence the other, I really don't have a choice.

Now, son, you know that's not accurate. You do have a choice. You can do what you want to do and what is most natural for you or...

Father, You know I am going to end up choosing what You want me to do.

Yes I do, but I still want you to choose.

Okay, I choose You, and I choose what You want me to do. How about I do a potential e-mail to him and run it by You first?

Sounds like a good plan. And son? I am proud of you. You are a good man and you have a good heart. Thanks for trusting Me.

Father, You are amazing. How do You do this? I felt like I "lost" on this, but now I feel so good. Thanks for Your affirmation and thanks for protecting me from myself.

Only God has 100 percent accurate perspectives customized to us. God's perspectives lift us above our situations. They exalt. Even if there is pain involved in them, it is surgical pain that brings healing. Our perspectives bring a pain that tends to damage and imprison us.

I regularly ask God for His perspective—I need it daily; He loves sharing it with me. Gaining His perspective has changed my life and greatly diminished the amount of grief I face.

Our Lord Jesus Christ says, "Come to me, all you who are weary and burdened, and I will give you rest. Take my yoke upon you and learn from me, for I am gentle and humble in heart, and you will find rest for your souls. For my yoke is easy and my burden is light" (Matthew 11:28-30). I believe one of the primary ways our Lord does this is by sharing with us His perspective—His thoughts—and then sharing with us His plan or His ways. You see, His yoke is easy, and after He takes on our burden, needless to say, it is exceedingly light.

Practice Session

Skills You're Acquiring and Practicing

- Gaining God's perspective
- Talking with God *relationally* through sharing emotions and receiving
- Engaging in back-and-forth dialogue with God

Your Assignment

Write two more dialogues with the Lord. In them, practice gaining God's perspective.

1. In the first dialogue, tell Him something you are concerned about or worried about. After you tell Him about it, tell Him your perspective (your interpretation) of it. Then ask God for His perspective: "God, Your thoughts are higher than mine. Will You tell me Your perspective?"

2. In your second dialogue, ask the Lord what He personally has for you through this book and the work you are doing to learn how to communicate with Him. Tell Him what effect this is having on you and how this seems to be affecting your relationship with Him. Ask Him for His perspective on these things.

Pointers

- *Interpretations, not events.* Remember that your perspective is your interpretation of the events, not the description of them and not a summary. Here's an example of sharing a problem with the Lord, then sharing your perspective:

  Father, I have a conference coming up next week, and I'm getting intimidated. I don't see how it can be anything but draining and time consuming. These things are full of schmoozing and networking, and You know that You just didn't make me to do that. And then I'm going to be buried when I get back to work and have a mile-high inbox waiting for me. I guess my perspective would be, "A crummy part of my job I'm not good at." Please give me Your perspective.

  God's perspective could be: "Part of your job where My strength is perfected in your weakness," or "Good opportunity for you to partner with Me."

- *Listen relationally.* Stay in the mode of a friend talking to a Friend or a child talking to your perfectly loving Father.

- *Let God speak.* Be aware of tendency to "hear" what you already know and fill in God's perspective for Him, such as, "My perspective is that this is 'A lesson you need to learn,'" or "My perspective is that you need to 'Trust Me'" or "My perspective is that 'All things work together for good.'"

- *Practice receiving*. After hearing from Him, please *receive* what He says. Allow it to sink in and affect you, and then tell Him how you feel about what He gives you.

Follow-up Coaching

Gaining God's perspective is a difficult area to coach you in because, even if I knew your situation and your perspective, I *don't know* God's perspective on it. And I want to avoid providing anything that might seem like a formula for gaining God's perspective. The whole point is that this is something we can't manufacture; we have to receive it from God.

So, I will give you some minimal direction and then send you back to keep practicing with God. Over the years, I have developed supreme confidence in Him: If you keep coming to Him and wanting to know His thoughts and be led by His Spirit, I *know* our Sovereign Shepherd and Father will share with you, lead you, and personally coach you (review chapter 4 if you'd like some encouragement in this).

1. Key indicators. I can't tell you for sure how to *know* you've gained God's perspective, but I can tell some indicators that you are doing well:

❑ You not only have God's thoughts, He also talks with you about His feelings toward you and your situation.

❑ You feel lightened and liberated when you hear God's perspective.

❑ God's perspective brings with it a sense of, "This is what righteousness must look and feel like." This brings you a sense of awe, especially if you are still stuck in the midst of a painful situation.

❑ God's perspectives are customized to you.

❑ Even if God's perspective brings correction or the possibility of pain or suffering, you feel helped and drawn closer to Him.

And here are some red flags that indicate you need to talk more with God about this:

❑ You can regularly predict God's perspective.

❑ You don't feel loved.

❑ Most of the time, God's perspective doesn't make you feel liberated or freed up.

❑ God's perspectives are general and could fit almost anyone.

❑ God's perspective often falls along the lines of misconceptions you've held about Him. (For example, if you believe God is like an indulgent grandfather, His perspectives never correct or speak of struggle or hardship. Or, if you tend to believe God's sole focus for you is to teach you life lessons, His perspectives are along the lines of "a time to learn through trials.")

Consider the practice you've done with perspectives against these two lists. Ask God to help you see if you have heard Him well. Also ask, "Is there anything I'm missing or anything else You would like to talk with me about here?" Write down what He tells you.

2. Continuing practice. For a great while, I practiced gaining God's perspective by drawing a grid like the one below on a piece of paper. Then I would regularly (several times in a week), write a sentence about my perspective on one side, then ask God for His perspective and fill it in on the other. This helped me greatly in learning to gain God's perspective. This week, try this exercise as you practice this key life skill.

If you tend to think visually, describe how you picture your situation. Then ask God to give you His accurate picture of what is really happening and show you how He is present in it.

My Perspective	God's Perspective

Advanced Assignment

For those wishing to advance further in learning how to accept God's perspective, look at what the Bible has to say about God's viewpoint of mistreatment, injustice, and unfairness. Please see appendix E if you are interested.

Review: Hearing from God

- You will grow in your skill at discerning His thoughts. Be willing to take the risk that you are hearing Him.
- Ask God to help you hear Him clearly, and to hear from only Him, not the enemy's interference or your own thoughts. Trust that your Father and Friend *wants* to communicate with you.

- Don't analyze away the thoughts that cross your mind. Write them down. You can always come back later and discern.
- Use a picture or scene if helpful (see appendix D).
- If you sense great blocks and/or confusion, revisit the follow-up coaching from chapter 5, and work through any necessary segments.
- If you get stuck, you can always go back to speculating what He would say by asking yourself, "If I had just said this to a perfect Father or outstanding Friend, how would He respond?"

Wrestling, Understanding, and Enjoying

By now I hope you're gaining some confidence as you dialogue with God and are beginning to talk with your loving Father in new and fresh ways. This is something I wish I had been taught as a young Christian.

I came to Christ in my teens, but finally began true growth in my 20s. I went to a church that gave me excellent Bible teaching and taught me how to study the Bible for myself. I was taught that growing as a Christian involved worshipping God, praying, studying the Bible, serving Him, and sharing my faith. As a typical male, I saw each area as tasks I needed to do if I wanted to be a true follower of Jesus Christ and I began being "responsible" in these areas. Though no one exactly said so, I thought doing these things constituted having a relationship with God.

All the disciplines I was taught are valid and valuable. However, I now see that having a *relationship* with God through Jesus Christ is truly just that—a *relationship!* Therefore learning and applying *relational* skills is essential.

125

Relationships—including ours with God—don't automatically develop depth and authenticity. Growing in these skills takes intentionality. If we are willing to press in and pursue relationship with God, to ask, seek, and knock, as Jesus told us to in Luke 11, we can experience an ever deepening and more authentic relationship with Him.

In chapter 6 we talked about the core relationship skill of building intimacy through sharing emotions and receiving. In this chapter, I'd like to talk about some relationship skills that will take your conversations to the next level, if you are willing to go there: wrestling with God, receiving and giving understanding, and enjoying God.

We'll begin with the skill of "wrestling." Now that you have some dialoguing experience with God, this skill will help you address deeper, more painful topics with Him.

WRESTLING WITH GOD

I heartily endorse "wrestling" with God—telling Him about our thoughts, emotions, and even disappointments with Him—pouring out our hearts in ways some might think irreverent or just not "allowed."

Many people initially think the whole idea of being this bold and upfront with God is sacrilegious. Since God is holy, perfect, and loving, on what basis would any of us presume to struggle with Him? Doesn't "fighting" with Him contradict faith and trust? Since we know we should always trust God, shouldn't we just keep our doubts and disappointments to ourselves and ask Him to give us better attitudes and help us be more trusting?

These are very good questions. But wrestling has biblical precedence. Perhaps the classic example is Jacob, who literally wrestles with God and "prevails." He is blessed at the end of the wrestling match this way: "Your name shall no longer be Jacob, but Israel, for you have striven with God and with men and have prevailed" (Genesis 32:28, NASB). Jacob responds, "I have seen God face to face, yet my life has been preserved" (verse 30). This is a significant moment in Jacob's life, truly a crossroads where God prepares Jacob to be His man and His leader. And God's perfect plan for this patriarch of our faith involved serious wrestling.

Most of the wrestling with God that we see in Scripture is not physical, but is more like wrestling as we will experience it: A "no holds barred" time when we pour out our hearts to God, sharing emotions that are messy, ugly, negative, and honest. We tell Him the thoughts and even judgments we are holding against Him, as inaccurate as they may be. We ask the questions burning in our hearts: "Why are You being so mean? Why don't You love me?" "Why don't You care about what is happening to me?" "I thought You said I could trust You, but I can't." "If this is how You love people, I don't think I am interested!"

We're not being sacrilegious or profane here; we're not cursing God or calling Him names. But we are being open and honest about our deepest struggles with Him. And we are not revealing anything new to Him; there is not a thought or feeling we will ever have that God is not fully aware of.

Did people in the Bible really do this? Without a doubt. We talk a lot about the "patience of Job" and miss that much of the book of Job is about Job struggling with his friends and eventually wrestling with God Himself. Listen to how Job wrestles with the injustice he is experiencing:

> Only grant me these two things, O God, and then I will not hide from you: Withdraw your hand far from me, and stop frightening me with your terrors. Then summon me and I will answer, or let me speak, and you reply.   (Job 13:20-22)

> Even today my complaint is bitter; [God's] hand is heavy in spite of my groaning. If only I knew where to find him; if only I could go to his dwelling! I would state my case before him and

fill my mouth with arguments. I would find out what he would answer me, and consider what he would say.   (Job 23:2-5)

Listen to how the Lord God Almighty chooses to respond to Job's questions, doubts, assumptions, and conclusions: "Then the LORD answered Job out of the storm. He said: 'Who is this that darkens my counsel with words without knowledge? Brace yourself like a man; I will question you, and you shall answer me'" (Job 38:1-3).

How would you like the Lord God to engage with you like that? Talk about heavy-duty wrestling! God obviously felt challenged and misrepresented. The Lord continues His response for all of chapters 38 and 39, and into chapter 40. His response was strong, but also consider what it *wasn't*: God didn't say Job sinned with his questions. God didn't punish Job. God didn't refuse to speak. God didn't strike Job dead. Most know the end of the story: Jehovah blessed Job even more than his beginning. God was greatly honored and glorified through Job, and one of the most righteous saints in our family lineage was exalted. Wrestling with God was an integral part of the process God used to purify Job's faith.

David, who I have already said is my favorite biblical person, is another example. David wrestled with God in ways I can only imagine. He was a man after God's own heart, and he knew God with an intimacy most Christians wish for. What I have found helpful is watching how David resolves so many conflicts through this struggling. Notice how David brazenly wrestles with the Lord:

How long, O LORD? Will you forget me forever? How long will you hide your face from me? How long must I wrestle with my thoughts and every day have sorrow in my heart? How long will my enemy triumph over me?   (Psalm 13:1-2)

My God, my God, why have you forsaken me? Why are you so far from saving me, so far from the words of my groaning?

O my God, I cry out by day, but you do not answer, by night, and am not silent. (Psalm 22:1-2)

I cry aloud to the LORD; I lift up my voice to the LORD for mercy. I pour out my complaint before him; before him I tell my trouble. (Psalm 142:1-2)

I believe a significant part of being a man or woman "after God's own heart" is the ability to pour out our hearts to Him like this—to take our concerns about Him *to* Him. I ask people wondering about this to read Psalms 44 and 88. I believe the primary purpose of these psalms is to model for us how God wishes us to pour out our hearts to Him when we are in great pain and wrestle with Him; these psalms are essential to the Bible.

Consider this example of wrestling. I have invited my daughter and now my granddaughter to wrestle with me when they disagree with me or when they are puzzled or hurt by my actions. I prefer this struggling be done with respect, but if my child or grandchild is confused and disillusioned and struggling because of me, I absolutely want them to share this with me. Even when they appear to be questioning or challenging something about my love or care or commitment to them, I still urge them to come and wrestle *with* me about it. I far prefer them "wrestling" over going off on their own to try to "fix" themselves or cutting off our relationship because of what they think may be true about me. I love them more than enough to be able to handle even something that may be hurtful to me. This is parental love and commitment, even from an imperfect human father and grandfather.

Once again, our Heavenly Father is a perfect, loving Father, the ultimate Father, the literal parental model for all fathers and mothers to follow. He is our faithful Friend who always and only has our best in mind and who never leaves or forsakes us. Wrestling with God is not only a biblical model but also something He encourages.

Listen to what it sounds like to wrestle with God over a deep grief.

Precious Lord, I want to meet with You. You are my Lord and my King and worthy of all of my praise. I do want to worship You, because You are so worthy. But Father, You know my heart is heavy and downcast. I don't know what to do with all these feelings. I feel so discouraged and hopeless.

Lord, I am torn up over not getting pregnant. You know all I've ever wanted is a good husband and to be a mommy, and I know You made me this way. I love kids.

Curt and I have tried *everything*. We waited patiently for so long and we didn't even pursue doctors for four years. We had our Sunday school class pray over us. I think all my friends are praying for me to get pregnant. Now I'm the only one without children. I don't think I can be a part of the children's ministry anymore because each time I am with the kids, it tears me up. Curt says it takes me days just to get back to "normal."

I did the right thing and didn't sleep around. I have always gone to church and I have served You in so many ways. I cannot understand why You would deny me the only thing I really want. I know You care about me but ... I just don't know what to say. So I am pouring my heart out to You and trying not to be disrespectful, but all I want is a baby. Why can't I have one?

Rebecca, you are My precious daughter. I know talking with Me like this and pouring out your heart is so hard for you. It means so much to Me that you would trust Me in such a vulnerable way. You are doing exactly what I want you to do. I know it feels like you are challenging Me, but you are not. You are just sharing the things closest to your heart with a Father who loves and adores you.

I know you don't understand. Like you said, I did make you to want children. I realize that all the women you are friends with have children and it seemed so easy for them. And then Ellen was so upset when she did get pregnant. I know how hard it is for you to work with children in the church, but you bring a smile to Me when I watch how you love them and enjoy teaching them about Me.

Sweetheart, I am allowing this trial, and I know it does not look like something a loving Father would do. You have a soft heart and you are a humble woman. You are willing to be My servant and allow Me to use you. Most of My girls are not like this.

I have things for you that you will find very fulfilling and rewarding. Part of My plan is for you to be able to talk with and minister to women exactly like where you are now. Think with Me for a minute.

You don't feel like you fit in with your friends, do you? Right now you believe that if you were pregnant you would be complete, that having a baby would bring you the joy and satisfaction you long for. Isn't this correct?

Yes, that's where I am.

My plan for you is to be complete and fulfilled whether you have children or not. I desire for you to experience joy and enjoyment now, not just when you have babies. Does this make sense to you, My daughter?

Yes, Father, it does and it's what I would want too. I just don't see how I could get there.

I know you can't see it yet. But I don't recall you praying about having joy or contentment or satisfaction now. You haven't asked Me for any of these things.

No I haven't. Even listening to You say these things scares me and makes me feel You are preparing me for no children, ever. So no, I really don't even want to ask you for joy or contentment now.

See, Rebecca, this is much of the problem. You want to trust Me but only as long as what I have for you matches up with what you think is best. Now let Me say this: I am not saying you won't have children. What I am saying is that My will for you (and how I wish to prepare you) is for you to have joy and satisfaction and some contentment right now; that I would be enough for you. Actually Curt would also love to feel that he is enough for you.

Then if I give you the desires of your heart, your joy will overflow. Or perhaps if I did not give you a child, your trust in Me would stay strong. Sweetheart, what I have for you is a wonderful and hard truth few of My kids ever really get— being content in whatever circumstance you find yourself in.

And the good news is that you and I are working together. I will never leave you alone and demand you work up joy or contentment on your own. With Me, you will learn this elusive secret that doesn't require a baby or a new home or a great vacation or kids that excel or more money in order to be "happy."

Father, I think I am understanding. I can't say I'm excited, but there is something about what You are telling me that touches me deeply. I want to say I believe You and trust You and I want to do this with You. But I'm just not sure I am there.

Wonderful! I am not asking you to be there. I would like to talk much more with you. I want to show you much more. I want you to know Me well and, because of that, love Me more and trust Me more. Your response delights me. I love you My daughter. Let's talk more. I do love you and I want to help you see and experience My love.

Thanks for this amazing talk, Father. I do love You and I do feel a lifting. Thanks for loving me and accepting me.

When you face suffering or struggle or disappointment with God, don't cut yourself off from Him or decide that because He didn't come through for you in the way you expected, you will no longer pray or perhaps even believe in Him. Don't choke because you are hurt and disappointed—how shallow such a relationship would be! Honestly share your pain and confusion and doubt; actually struggle with our Lord and Master. Then listen to Him. Allow Him to share His feelings and His thoughts and His perspective with you. Share more of yourself and tell Him how His response makes you feel. Listen to Him again. Struggle some more. Gradually, He will amaze you as He patiently leads you to an eventual resolution, perhaps in one dialogue, usually through many.

The topics you're wrestling about are rarely simple or easy, so the resolution can take some time. God is so gracious; He doesn't lower the boom on you and expect you to get with the program. He doesn't say, "Buck up and get your attitude right." It is always, "Let Me help you. We can do this." He sees it as His job to help you deal with extremely difficult things. He listens, responds, shares tough truths, gives you compassion, and helps you move closer to Him relationally over time. He respects the depth of your struggle as He invites you to continue to engage with Him.

Will you go deep with Him in this way He prescribes and models?

GIVING AND RECEIVING UNDERSTANDING

Another relationship skill that will move your conversations with God to a new level is that of giving and receiving understanding.

"Understanding" is a foundational communication skill in all relationships. For sure, in order for our marriages to be healthy, we husbands better be skillful at communicating understanding to our wives. But this is also a foundational parenting skill. In order not to exasperate our children, as Ephesians 6:4 commands, we *must* give them understanding.

When I have counseled families with a teen who is labeled "out of control," the first thing I do is give the teen understanding. These teens do not feel their parents understand them *at all*. So I listen carefully, regardless of how off base their perceptions may be. I give them understanding by "entering into" their experience with them. I let them know I have heard what they are saying and give them words of care and affirmation: "So you really think this is unfair and unreasonable for any parent to ask of a kid. That has to be pretty frustrating and discouraging, when someone who says they care about you won't even listen to you." I recognize how bad it feels to experience what they are experiencing. Then I ask them how they would deal with their son or their daughter in a similar situation. I am amazed at how rational and sane teens can be once they feel understood and respected.

From here we negotiate some temporary boundaries and consequences. Many of these actually come from the teen. And I insist to the parents that for the next few weeks, in any conversation, the teen gets to speak first. The parents must listen to what the teen is saying and give understanding by repeating back what they have heard, until the teen says, "I feel understood." Only then can the parents speak and share their thoughts, with the teen listening and repeating back until the parents can say, "I feel understood."

Though this is just a beginning to the counseling process, amazingly, after some weeks of giving understanding, many families do not come for more counseling. I know what you may be thinking: *No wonder, they probably decided to go to a real counselor who knows how to deal with these problems!* Actually, many report that, miraculously, their teens are no longer "out of control." Though that doesn't happen with all families, it is surprising that something so simple as making sure another person feels understood can carry such power.

Because giving understanding is such a foundational communication skill, we should expect to experience it in our conversations with God. God is the absolute best at giving understanding. Once I began anticipating and looking for God's understanding, I made some fascinating discoveries. I'd thought I was a typical male and didn't need much understanding as long as people treated me decently and did as they should. However, I discovered I *like* receiving understanding. When God gives me His exceptional understanding, I find it wonderful. I feel affirmed, cared for, and important. When He adds a touch of empathy, such as, "I know this is really hard. No wonder you are feeling frustrated and unsure," I find myself enthusiastically saying, "Exactly!" Feeling understood *feels good.*

Plus, it is impossible for God to give us understanding without communicating care. Every time God gives understanding, He always gives it along with His care. Part of the reason receiving understanding is so good is that we finally feel deeply understood and cared for. Learning to make space for and receive God's understanding is an invaluable relationship skill.

But understanding goes two ways: Not only do we want to receive God's understanding, we also want to give *Him* understanding. When a good friend shared this idea with me for the first time, it took me a bit by surprise because I'd not thought about giving God *my* understanding. I had been taught that God is all-sufficient; He needs nothing. Then I remembered Abraham being called the "friend of God." I've always thought I would love to hear God refer to me as His friend. But now, as I thought about the place that giving and receiving understanding plays in a relationship, I was feeling like maybe I hadn't been such a good friend to the Lord. Try to imagine a friendship with someone who never gives you any understanding or compassion or care. Unfortunately many of us can think of such a relationship. It's not very satisfying, is it?

When I first saw the movie *The Passion of Christ,* I felt great compassion and grief and heartbreak as I saw the Lord Jesus beaten and whipped and persecuted. I wept with God over this. Yet even then, most of my feelings came from the thought, *You must love me in an incredible way to suffer like that for me.* I realized I still had a way to go to grieve with my Father over how it must have felt for Him, as a father, to see His Son endure such excruciating pain yet not intervene. So I began to watch for times when I could relate with God by considering what He experiences and giving Him understanding.

Once, I saw a TV report showing a young teen girl getting beaten up and kicked repeatedly by two other girls, like she was nothing—while a security guard stood nearby, doing nothing. I was so disturbed; in the past I might have prayed for her, but now I talked about it with my Lord. I told Him how much it disturbed me, but also told Him I could only imagine how it must tear at His heart and grieve and disturb Him to see His precious daughter being treated worse than we would treat the least of animals: "This is so hard for me, but how was it for You to watch that happen? That girl is someone You love, not just a random stranger whom You've never met."

Or when I see the hatred some people feel toward God's children, I go beyond just considering how it makes me feel. I engage with my Father, see things more through His eyes, understand His feelings, and give Him understanding.

I now also do this when He is overjoyed; I love looking at things from His perspective and sharing in His joy—over a lost child coming to Him, over seeing a son or daughter open up and share something when they have hidden themselves for so long, over seeing someone giving greatly of his time with no chance of any personal gain, all for the sake of the Name of Jesus Christ.

And when I read Scripture, I consider what is happening from God's point of view and share how it must have hurt Him when His people refused to listen to Him.

Our Father has shared with me how much this means to Him; how rare it is for Him to have a son or daughter who gives Him understanding, who cares for Him in this way. Please do this with our Father.

Here is an example of a young father whose experience with his daughter helped him see God's heart and allowed him to give God understanding:

Father, if nothing else, this experience has shown me that our daughter really loves us. She cannot just say that yet, but she is demonstrating to us that she wants to be with us and loves us. It even allows me to reflect on our relationship. It must sadden You when we leave You or do not want to be with You.

This experience for you is an invaluable lesson. I covet My time with you and when you do not want to meet with Me, I am saddened because I have so much for you, and I want to comfort you, and just be with you. I love My time with you and clearly your daughter loves her time with her daddy.

Can you see how meaningful this is to our Father?

ENJOYING GOD

Finally, we can take our conversations with God to another level by learning how to enjoy Him. My experience has been that most Christians rarely think about enjoying God, and even fewer intentionally pursue such times. Yet I do not have a close relationship where we don't enjoy each other. Actually I cannot imagine how a relationship *could* be close and meaningful without enjoying each other. It doesn't occur to most of us that enjoying each other is important to our Father.

When we look at various definitions of *enjoy*, we can put them together and realize that enjoying means we feel or perceive with pleasure, experience with joy, and possess with satisfaction, pleasure, and delight. This understanding is congruent with these truths from God's Word:

You have made known to me the path of life; you will fill me with joy in your presence. (Psalm 16:11)

> Instruct those who are rich in this present world not to be conceited or to fix their hope on the uncertainty of riches, but on God, who richly supplies us with all things to enjoy.
>
> (1 Timothy 6:17, NASB)

But my favorite is Zephaniah 3:17: "The LORD your God is with you, he is mighty to save. He will take great delight in you, he will quiet you with his love, he will rejoice over you with singing." What an outstanding picture to enjoy and talk over with our Lord!

Here are just a few of the ways my Father and Friend has taught me to enjoy Him:

- Talking to Him about exciting news and things that are special to me
- Enjoying His beauty in nature, music, and art and letting Him tell me why these things are special to Him
- Discovering something with Him
- Working on a project together in the way He desires
- Taking an intentional retreat with Him—just me and Him
- Singing to Him; amazingly, my quality of singing isn't important to Him (or maybe that's why He finds my singing enjoyable!)
- Being silent with Him, especially in the beauty of His creation
- Talking with Him; joking with Him; receiving His teasing
- Noticing and enjoying His unique sense of humor
- Reminiscing with Him
- Having Him teach me from His Word in a leisurely fashion
- Celebrating His blessings and special answers to prayer
- Laughing with Him

Please ask God to show you what He has for you in enjoying Him and receiving His pleasure and delight of you. Include Him in your celebrations; share good things with Him when they happen. When a child does something amazing and delightful, don't just call a friend or family member and share your joy; also "call" God and talk with Him. When you're laughing over something, see if He wants to laugh with you. When you're calling up a friend to tell good news, talk to God too. When you find a great new restaurant, let God know how much you enjoy it and why it was special to you.

Ask what He enjoys doing and do that with Him. Find out what He likes to talk and laugh about, and share this with Him. Ask Him what He's doing right now that He's really enjoying, and then enjoy the experience with Him.

Here is an example of how one of my friends enjoyed God:

I love You so much, Abba Father. I am so glad the past has been forgiven!

What past? LOL!

Ok, You are right! I don't need to dwell on it. Wow, did You just say LOL? That's funny.

I know your language! Why would that surprise you?

Because You are so full of surprises that it catches me off guard.

I find joy in surprising you with goodness.

WORTH THE EFFORT

Wrestling with God, giving and receiving understanding, enjoying God—learning these three skills and being deliberate about including them in our dialogues with God can feel awkward and uncomfortable, but the payoff is always worth it.

You can't go to any depth in a relationship, much less one with God, without engaging in these skills. They are essential relationship components for all relationships. If you don't have a way to have conflict and wrestle in a relationship, all you can do is be superficial. If you can't touch the other person relationally and have an impact on them by giving and receiving understanding, all you have is a surface relationship. And a relationship without shared enjoyment is not much of a relationship.

These skills also work together. It may seem possible to enjoy someone and never wrestle with that person. But if you don't know how to engage in conflict together, you can only enjoy a few common shared interests. You can't enjoy each other on a much deeper level. On the other hand, if you only wrestle with someone and never enjoy that person, then what an awful relationship that is! Why be in it?

If you take the time to invest yourself in learning and applying these skills to your relationship and conversations with God, you will discover God in ways you did not know possible. You will make a connection to the God of the Bible in ways many people miss. You will be able to know God experientially, not just intellectually or cognitively; maybe even be *His* friend!

Practice Session

Skills You're Acquiring and Practicing

- Wrestling with God
- Giving and receiving understanding
- Enjoying God
- Being "yourself" with God (Share emotions. Be honest. Take risks. Laugh.)

Your Assignment

Write two more dialogues with the Lord. Continue gaining His perspective.

1. In the first dialogue, try wrestling with God. If this is the first time you've trusted God enough to wrestle with Him, don't go to the extreme yet—for example, don't yet talk about a massive life disappointment that almost caused you to turn away from the faith. For now, wrestle over something where you feel at odds with Him or where you have been somewhat disappointed or feel kind of neglected.

2. In your second dialogue, try your hand at enjoying God, using one of the following suggestions.

- Tell Him about something funny that happened to you in the past week.
- Talk about something you enjoyed doing in the past week.
- Tell Him something about Him you really like, and ask Him what He likes or enjoys about you.
- Share something that really tickles you with the Lord and why it is fun to you. (I recently did this with the Abbott and Costello comedy bit, "Who's on First.")
- Ask God what activity you both enjoy that He would like to do with you.

Pointers for Your Wrestling Dialogue

- *Use emotion words.* Wrestling is very relational. Be sure to tell God how you are feeling. Be open to God sharing His emotions with you as well.

- *Let God be God.* He may not want to talk about what you bring up. He may not directly answer you. His "answer" may not feel satisfying. Respond to whatever He says … keep the conversation going.

- *Persevere and press in.* Sometimes when you're wrestling with God, you're getting into areas of conversation that are fairly emotional and painful. It can be harder to hear from God in the middle of all this emotion. Give yourself time for these conversations; don't rush them. Keep risking that you *are* hearing God and keep the conversation going.

If you feel a mocking, condemning, battering, or contemptuous tone coming through in "God's" voice, simply say, "Father, I feeling like this is what's happening _____, and that maybe the enemy is trying to interfere with what we're talking about. I know You want Your sheep to hear You and only You. Holy Spirit, I truly want to hear from only You—not my mind, not my emotions, not my misconceptions of You, and not from the enemy. Will You clear away any distractions and enable me to hear clearly?" Then keep the conversation going.

Follow-up Coaching

I will give you coaching for both of your dialogues, but first let me make a general note: When you are learning these more advanced relational skills with God, your misconceptions of Him may come into play. Be aware of the misconceptions you are prone to and let God talk with you about them.

Your "Wrestling" Dialogue

Wrestling can be a new skill for many of us; for others it comes naturally. The dialogue you have done here may just be the beginning of a process with God.

1. Key indicators. If you were able to wrestle with God, take a look back at your dialogue. You're doing well if

❑ You have given God raw, unedited, pain and struggles.

- ❑ You have fully expressed yourself, both feelings and thoughts.

- ❑ You've said the things that seem to be unmentionable.

- ❑ God has heard, received, and responded to you in ways that astound you. You feel understood, accepted, and respected.

- ❑ You've gained His perspective, which was far different from yours.

- ❑ You've engaged with God in a process (likely the first dialogue of several) toward resolving these issues and advancing your relationship.

If you feel uncertain how to proceed, ask God how He would like to keep talking about the issue where you are struggling. Write down what He tells you.

2. Blocked or unable to wrestle. If you're uncomfortable with the idea of wrestling with God, do another dialogue and talk with Him about it. Ask Him how He wants to relate with you. Here are some ways you might get started:

- "God, I'm really skeptical of the whole idea of wrestling with You. It doesn't feel right to talk to You in those ways. How will You feel if I try to wrestle with You?"

- "Friend, I don't know if wrestling is really a part of friendship with You. It's not something I do with my friends. Do you really want me to talk with You like that?"

- "Father, I have to be honest: Wrestling with You scares me. I'm ready to respect and obey You but not to question You or challenge You. Is this really something You want to do with Your children?"

Your "Enjoying" Dialogue

For this dialogue, I'd like to introduce you to the idea of God as your ideal coach. Long after this course is finished, I hope you will continue to talk with Him and ask Him to help you discern if you are hearing accurately from Him.

1. **God as your Coach.** Ask God the following questions, and record His replies.

a.   Father and Friend, what did You particularly like or appreciate about this dialogue?

b.   Is there anything You would want to change or add?

c.   Is there anything else in this conversation that You want to point out or want me to pay attention to?

FACILITATING GOD'S INITIATION

I f you're a parent, imagine that the only way you can communicate with your children is when they start a conversation with you. And even then, you can only talk about what they bring up; you can't introduce any topics into the conversation. How would that be?

You're probably laughing at the thought! Many—if not most—of our conversations with our children are about things they would definitely never bring up, such as schoolwork or loving their siblings or serving others. Goodness, if we could not initiate conversations with our children, good parenting would cease!

A similar truth exists with our Heavenly Father. Much of what He wants and needs to talk about with us could never begin with us. Often, that is not because we would rather *not* talk about something but because we aren't aware of what we need to know or consider or be warned of. So as you begin to talk regularly with God, it's important that you let Him initiate topics with you.

I want to help you learn to let God direct your conversations with Him so you can discuss the topics He longs to bring up with you and so He can parent you perfectly. Facilitating God's initiation is an advanced skill, but it is also one of the most essential ones if we are going to be about furthering God's kingdom and battling forces we cannot see and living the abundant life Jesus desires for us.

I have found this important skill is developed much like the more basic ones we have discussed: It requires deliberate effort and practice. You see, most Christians don't expect God to initiate; they are surprised when it happens. So they rarely think to open up the conversation and see if God has anything to talk about. A key shift happens when we begin to *expect* the Lord to initiate and talk about things that are important to Him.

LEARNING TO LET GOD INITIATE

I have found that asking God questions helps immeasurably to change my expectations of Him and give Him a chance to introduce topics He'd like to talk with me about.

Over the years, I have asked God many different kinds of questions to facilitate His initiation. I'm going to describe quite a few, but I am not expecting you to ask them all at once or in every dialogue. Instead, I am going to give examples you can draw from, one by one, to allow God to speak about what's on His heart and mind for you. The first question, "What do you want today?" lets God speak into your upcoming day.

"What Do You Want Today?"

Years ago I chose to start each day with three questions:

1. Lord, what do You want me to do today?
2. What do You want to do in me?
3. What do You want to do through me?

In my experience, even when I ask all three of these questions, God usually picks one to focus on.

My job often consists of prescheduled meetings with people. Therefore, asking, "What do You want me to do today?" seems somewhat unnecessary; my calendar is showing me what I have to do. But even though God doesn't often alter my schedule (sometimes He does), the Lord shows me that each day has the potential for eternal value.

For example, He might say, "Today is going to be a tough day. I am using this as a trial. It's a chance to work through how to have joy in the midst of a day like this. Don't worry; I'm going to be doing this with you, and we can talk it over during the day and after you're done."

Or, "Today I want you to focus on your wife and help her feel loved and important to you." My first reaction to that is often, "Lord, I have seven meetings back to back; today is packed. I don't have time for such an assignment!" But He has shown me He doesn't necessarily mean altering my scheduled work day. When He gives me a day like this, I call Letty during a break and tell her I'm thinking about her. Sometimes I share specific thoughts of appreciation and then say, "Could we have lunch together and go to that restaurant you like?" or, "I want to take you out tonight for dinner. I was thinking you might enjoy Chinese food." Let me just say this. Doing something like this *makes* my wife's day—and my Father knows that. He can easily show me how to accomplish what He wants me to do in spite of my work schedule.

When I ask, "What do You want to do in me today?" He may say, "I want you to enjoy working with Me today. I want to be Your partner and show you some things you will find interesting." Obviously, if I choose to accept this invitation, my day will be radically different from whatever I could accomplish and experience on my own.

Or He may say, "Today will try your patience. I want to develop patience in you. Trust Me to help you with the annoying parts." I am amazed how this initiation changes what would have been an awful day into one that's difficult but rewarding.

Finally, when I ask, "What do You want to do through me?" our Father often says, "Today I want you to concentrate on making everyone you meet with feel valued and important." This alters how I start meetings or the manner in which I deal with difficulties or conflicts. People usually thank me after meetings on days when God has said this to me!

Or the Lord may say, "In your two o'clock meeting today, you will encounter some real resistance. Before you try to deal with the conflict, ask how this person is doing. Show concern and interest. This person needs someone to talk to and someone just to care." Do I need to say how these types of meetings go?

During seasons when I have started my day with these three questions, I usually do it with a partner or two who is using the same questions. We will meet from time to time and talk about how it is going and what we are learning about ourselves and about the Lord. I find it intriguing to record God's focus for me each day and then look back and observe clear themes He emphasized during the month.

"Do You Have Any Personal Messages for Me?"

Another way to assist receiving God's initiation is to ask Him, "Do you have any personal messages for me?" As a male, I am not inclined to ask this type of question. However, God has shown me that I am His son or, as He sometimes says, His boy. I am and always will be "His boy."

I may not admit it or even recognize it, but I do need and want my Heavenly Father's affection and approval. When He says, "Way to go, son," I do smile. When He says, "I really enjoyed you today," I'm happy and grateful. When He says, "I am with you and I am for you," nothing pleases and encourages me more. I never grow tired of hearing Him say these things. Or when He says, "I am so glad you are My son, My boy," I realize I need to hear these things; they touch me deeply.

When I consider that few Christians ever hear these essential words from their Father, it truly grieves me. It is not because God is not thinking or saying these truths; it is because so many of God's sons and daughters do not know how to hear or receive the incredible words of blessing He has for each one of us.

"What Sins Do I Need to Confess?"

This question sounds intimidating and maybe even frightening, but again, consider who we are asking. If our children came and asked in humility, "Mom or Dad, do you see anything in my life right now that is not right?" is there any chance we would withhold our input? Furthermore, we would probably try to talk in a gentle, kind, and compassionate way.

Our Heavenly Father is a perfect, loving parent. If we ask Him, "What sins do I need to confess?" He will reveal what we need to see and what we need to confess. If we confess and agree with Him, He will immediately wash us and cleanse us and separate our sins from us as far as the east is from the west.

Being corrected and disciplined in the loving, creative way that our perfect Heavenly Father uses with us is unique. Most of us may have experienced a touch of this in our lives and many of us have, on occasion, given correction and discipline in this fashion. But few of us have experienced correction and discipline in a loving, creative way with great regularity, and few of us have been able to give this with any consistency.

I am in my 60s and have watched the Lord correct and discipline me and many others with affection, love, grace, and even humor. He is forceful when necessary, but not harsh or condemning. Yet when I witness this or experience it for myself, I am often still blown away. I am astounded that the Lord God is the almighty, majestic, transcendent, infinite God and King of the universe, and yet He is my gentle, kind Father who disciplines and corrects me with unconditional love and tenderhearted care. How He balances all these attributes is beyond me and compels me to worship and adore Him. The way He dispenses grace and mercy and forgiveness is masterful and inspiring. Truly, He draws us with His love!

"What Tendencies Do I Have That Grieve and Quench Your Spirit?" or "Is There a Way Today or Yesterday That I Quenched or Grieved Your Spirit?"

We grieve and quench the Holy Spirit when we shut out His ability to speak to us, to guide us, to redirect us, to convict us. We each have our personalized ways of doing this. My experience is that most of us don't know what those ways are because we have not asked. Actually most of us have never even thought about this. If we ask, God will disclose our specific tendencies that grieve and/or quench Him.

The most classic way we quench the Holy Spirit is with our independence. God might say, "Do you realize we have never talked about _____ and yet this area is somewhat consuming you?" Or He may say, when we are entrenched in one of our self-defeating patterns, "Son/daughter you do know I am here with you? I see what is happening; let's talk."

Maybe He would say, "How about you and I talk about how you and your spouse are doing? Are you aware of how he/she is feeling right now? You know you are wrong, but you just can't admit it, can you? This stubbornness and unwillingness to let someone help you is grieving Me. This is not what I want. Let's do something about this."

Or He might say, "Do you remember hearing at church about that family and their need for someone to come in and help? Well, that's something you're really good at, yet it didn't even cross your mind to reach out to them. This is quenching My Spirit. I want to use you."

Maybe He'll want to talk about the spiritual gift He personally picked for you and how it is lying dormant. This negligence could be quenching Him, if not actively grieving Him.

Or maybe you're reading or studying the Bible in your own effort. If you have no concept of asking the Holy Spirit to show you God's truth and what He has for you personally, then you are quenching the ministry of the Holy Spirit. Essentially, you're saying, "*I* need to figure this out." God is saying, "It was never my plan for you to figure out My Word. That's My job. I want to speak with you, reveal My truth to you, and impart life to you through it."

In chapter 4 we considered a long list of what the Holy Spirit does with us. If we're not experiencing those things, then something is blocking our relationship. If we ask God to expose blocks and hindrances, He will gladly and gracious reveal them to us.

"What Should I See?"

Another way I attempt to be open to the Lord's initiating is by asking Him, "What do You want me to see that I don't see?"

Try to imagine one of your kids asking you, "Mom, Dad, do you have any concerns about me at this time? What do you see in me that I don't see?" Granted, this is clearly an imaginary situation! But if something like this did happen, would you be willing to share your genuine concerns with your son or daughter? Or if one of your friends asked you, "Do you see any self-defeating or unhealthy patterns in me that are blocking or hindering me?" wouldn't you share with your friend? Absolutely! The same is true of our Heavenly Father and Friend.

Sometimes when I ask my Father what I need to see, He shares with me that I am too goal-oriented right now and I need to be more relational. Or He says I am not giving my wife or daughter sufficient focused attention or engaging in things that are important to them. Maybe He says I have gotten too competitive in my exercising and relaxing time and therefore I'm not receiving any restorative benefit from the hobbies I enjoy.

He may say I am procrastinating on that project I am not looking forward to, but if I will work on it today, He will bless me. Or He may say I am avoiding someone I am annoyed with. I could go on and on. My Father seems to have ample opportunities to help me see what I need to see!

Receiving this kind of input from God may sound stressful, but what I have experienced is that He really does know what is best for me. When I pay attention to His concerns, I always end up in a better place. My stress level goes down; the people I love actually *feel* loved; I get more work done; things don't build up as much around me or in me; I enjoy life more; I feel like my life is in order and balanced and working well.

In addition, our Father also shares with us about long-standing issues we need to be aware of. Here is what Oswald Chambers says about understanding ourselves: "We have to get rid of the idea that we understand ourselves, it is the last conceit to go. The only One who understands us is God."[1] I believe this is brilliant insight.

As a licensed professional counselor, much of my education focused on understanding men and women and helping them understand themselves. Yet I truly believe that if anyone wants to understand himself, his strengths and weaknesses, and his self-defeating patterns, our Heavenly Father is the only One who has complete and accurate information and can dispense it effectively. Anyone who chooses to receive His initiation in these areas will be given His superior insight along with His excellent parenting. God may also ask you to share some of these things with someone else and accept help and support. Fortunately this advanced level of self-understanding is accessible to every one of God's sons and daughters.

Take, for example, the question, "God, what do I need to see about this fear that seems to paralyze me?" He may show us deep beliefs that support a lifestyle of fear. Sometimes He shows us past events that traumatized us and have kept us in a dwarfed state. Many times we have core negative emotions that virtually guarantee self-defeat—emotions like feeling abandoned, abused, worthless, unlovable, or helpless.

Or, when we ask Him what we need to see, He may reveal our inaccurate thought patterns. Sometimes these are subconscious, which obviously creates great problems; how can we deal with something we do not know? Thoughts such as, "I will never amount to anything good," "No one will ever love me," "I am damaged goods," "I can never escape the terrible things I have done," "I am alone, I am all by myself." How are we to discover thoughts like these that are somewhat hidden in our minds?

The great news is that these penetrating insights require no great effort for our God; they are instantly accessible to Him. Imagine the hope that comes with the realization that these patterns can be discovered and disclosed, as well as treated with God's care and wisdom. How sad that things like this imprison us, especially when we have a God who delights in freeing us from all that enslaves us.

If we ask Him to show us what we need to see so we can look more and more like the Lord Jesus and be good reflectors of His image and His glory, our God will reveal to us unparalleled understanding and insight. He is remarkable! I love this promise from our Father that the apostle Paul writes, "For I am confident of this very thing, that He who began a good work in you will perfect it until the day of Christ Jesus" (Philippians 1:6, NASB). God's exceptional and personal parenting blossoms in those who know how to communicate with Him and receive His initiation.

"What Do You Have for Me from Your Word?"

My plan is never again to read or study the Bible without first asking God to speak to me about what He has for me. He has so much to say. His Word truly is alive and powerful. I like to ask Him, "What do You have for me in this passage? What do You want me to see or learn or understand?" A. W. Tozer is one of my favorite writers. Listen to what he says:

Sound Bible exposition is an imperative *must* in the Church of the Living God. Without it no church can be a New Testament church in any strict meaning of that term. But exposition may be carried on in such way as to leave the hearers devoid of any true spiritual nourishment whatever. For it is not mere words that nourish the soul, but God Himself, and unless and until the hearers find God in personal experiences they are not the better for having heard the truth. The Bible is not an end in itself, but a means to bring men to an intimate and satisfying knowledge of God, that they may enter into Him, that they may delight in His Presence, may taste and know the inner sweetness of the very God Himself in the core and center of their hearts.[2]

I want to know and experience the Lord like this!

Recently I was teaching from Isaiah 55:1-3. The Lord focused me on what He is asking for in these verses: He wants us to come and listen. But then He asked me to notice that He does not ask us to bring anything or prepare in any way to come and meet with Him. This struck me. It is extremely unusual for me to meet with someone of importance, even if I am mainly coming to listen, and not prepare in *any* way. The more I meditated about this in the Lord's presence the more impressed I was. I felt compelled to ask Him, "Do You have any applications for me from this passage?" He showed me He would *prefer* I don't bring anything; that anything I bring would not help in any way and that He would *prefer* I not prepare, but just come to Him. I love the way He teaches, and I love to sit with Him in His classroom. It still amazes me that He is willing to hold class for just me!

Another question I really like asking is, "What do You want me to enjoy from Your Word?" Again from my study of Isaiah 55, the Lord revealed that He shows His heart in the promise, "Listen, listen to Me, and eat what is good, and your soul will delight in the richest of fare" (verse 2). He is not willing to give me only what I need; His heart is for me to receive "the richest of fare," the best of the best! Wow, our Father is amazing!

God has so very much for us in His written Word. Even when I come to passages I have studied and taught a dozen times, the Lord always has something new for me. I feel like saying, "How do You *do* that?" But, after all, He is God.

"How Shall I Pray?"

I have always deeply appreciated the truth that the Holy Spirit intercedes for me when I do not know how to pray (Romans 8:26); obviously God knows how best to pray for me and for others. But if God really knows how best to pray for everyone and if He wants me to pray for others, then certainly He would want me to know how best to pray. So when I pray for concerns or for other people, I ask Him, "How do you want me to pray?" Oswald Chambers says,

> Intercession means that we rouse ourselves up to get the mind of Christ about the one for whom we pray.[3]

> True intercession involves bringing the person, or the circumstance that seems to be crashing in on you, before God, until you are changed by His attitude toward that person or circumstance … It is having His mind and His perspective.[4]

When I pray for others, I want God's thoughts and ways, not mine. I want His perspective and His will for all I pray for. For example, instead of praying for healing from an illness, which would be my instinct, at times I have found the Lord directing me to pray for someone to find the Lord and His power and His peace in the midst of this illness. Then imagine my excitement upon hearing how the Lord revealed Himself to this person in the illness, got his attention, and touched him in a powerful way, so that he trusted God instead of just waiting for the illness to be removed. Then to hear how this affected his relationship with God as well as how God used his testimony to encourage others—at times like this I am so grateful I listen to God before starting intercessory prayer.

Another time in a marriage situation, instead of praying for a husband to get his act together and deal with a sinful pattern, which is how I wanted to pray, God directed me to pray for a different outcome. He told me to pray that the man's sin would become known, that he would have to face the consequences, and that through a time of humiliation and brokenness, God would capture this man for Himself.

The end of the story: This man's sin was exposed, he was humiliated and broken, the future of his marriage was questionable, his relationship with his children was greatly tested and at risk. But God did capture this man, and now he speaks out of his brokenness to other men; his marriage is stronger than at any other point, and his children now respect their dad and want to be around him. Again, God allowed me to be a part of an amazing story. This very different intercessory prayer helped change lives and altered the entire direction of this family. Can you see why now I will only do "listening" intercessory prayer?

Now, as I use my communicating with God skills and simply ask the Lord to show me how best to pray, I am amazed with what He shows me. Even though I wouldn't say I am gifted in intercessory prayer, God is. And as He shares His intercession with me, I have discovered I can pray in partnership with Him and in great power.

"What Do You Want to Talk About?"

An easy way to seek the Lord's initiation is simply to ask, "Lord, what would You like to bring up or address or discuss with me?" Because this question lacks any context, it can be more difficult to hear God's answer here, so I would not suggest starting with this question. Gain experience with the other questions first. But when I do ask this, the Lord tells me how much He appreciates this "freedom." He says few of His kids show this kind of respect or trust. I know when I ask friends or family members what they would like to talk about, most appreciate the opportunity. Some even note how unusual it is to be asked. That's kind of a shame, isn't it? I don't want to have conversations with people I care about and only talk about what I want to talk about or just trust they will be selfish enough, like I am, to interrupt me and bring up what they want to talk about. Plus, I do want to know what others would like to talk about and what they are interested in.

When I have asked the Lord what He wants to talk about, I am often surprised. Today, He wanted to talk about the Olympics, which are being held as I write. Recently He said He would like to talk about the discussion Letty and I had over our concern for a friend. Sometimes He says He would like to discuss a particular passage of Scripture with me (I always find this pretty cool because, when He brings up a reference, I often don't remember what passage it is).

Sometimes He brings up a worry I have that I am not fully aware of. This makes me feel cared for and very understood. Sometimes He wishes to discuss something I enjoyed or that meant something to me. When I begin talking it over with Him, most times I discover something interesting about myself.

Sometimes He wants to talk about a mutual friend. Sometimes He even gives me words to speak to this friend. (Most people really appreciate this.) The possibilities are endless. The more I ask open-ended questions like this, the more interesting, exciting, intriguing, and fun I find our Lord to be.

The Lord's Prayer

I have given you many examples of the kinds of questions you can ask that allow God to initiate with you. But I also want to remind you to use the Lord's model prayer as a foundation for questions, as we talked about in chapter 3. Sometimes I use only one of the questions below in a day; sometimes I use several. But I always make sure to pause and give the Lord space to initiate a conversation about any of these areas.

Hallowed (set apart) be your name ...
"Which of your attributes or names do you want to set apart or make known to me today?" (e.g., Counselor, King, Wisdom, Justice, Kindness)

Your kingdom come, your will be done ...
"How do You want Your Kingdom to rule and reign in me and in my life today?"

Give me today my daily bread ...
"What is Your portion for me today?"

Forgive my sins as I forgive those who sin against me ...
"What do I need to confess today? Is there anyone I need to forgive?"

Lead me away from temptation and deliver me from evil ...
"How will I be tempted today?"
"What are Satan's schemes against me for today?"
"How would you like to rescue me from myself or from the enemy?"

Whether you ask these questions or any of the others in this chapter, you are allowing God to take charge of your conversations.

When God initiates a conversation, He will often want to follow up and continue it. So expect Him to return to the topic and want to talk more about it with you later. Please leave the door open for this and allow Him the opportunity to direct His time with you.

TRUE FOLLOWERS

Jesus Christ is not our consultant; He is our master, king, ruler, boss—the head of our lives. His is not a passive position; anyone who is ruling and reigning has a lot to initiate and communicate.

And there is no father—especially a father of young children (and isn't that what we all are with God?)—who doesn't initiate. If a parent never initiates, what kind of parenting is that? A good parent brings up things you'd never talk about or that would never occur to you.

When God initiates with us, we experience God really being God in our lives. We become dependent on Him. We become actual followers and disciples.

I love God's initiation, because He knows everything and He's all powerful and He's present everywhere. Not to meet with and listen to Someone with all this and who also wants the best for me ... well, that would not be smart!

Practice Session

Skills You're Acquiring and Practicing

- Allowing God the opportunity to initiate topics and conversations
- Relating with God through receiving from Him, sharing emotions, giving and receiving understanding, wrestling, and enjoying

Your Assignment

Do another dialogue with God. Choose one of the questions from this chapter to ask Him. To start with, choose one of the more specific questions rather than a wide-open question. This provides some context and can make it easier to discern what God is saying. Please share your heart with Your Father and Friend and then listen to Him speak.

Pointers

- *Allow space for God to answer* even if you feel the uncertainty of "waiting" to hear Him. Take the risk to write down what you think you are hearing, without over-analyzing.

- *Ask God follow-up questions* rather than assume you know what He means. For example, if you were to ask, "What do you want to provide for me today," and God answered, "My joy," follow up on that. You could ask, "Is there a certain aspect of your joy I especially need?" or, "How would you like me to experience it?" or, "Why do I need joy?" Give God space to tell you more than a phrase or a sentence, if He wants to.

Follow-up Coaching

Facilitating God's initiation is a valuable skill, but a more advanced one. You can expect to grow in it as you grow in trusting and hearing from God. Also consider that if you truly learn how to listen to God's initiation, Satan has lost a great hold over you. Therefore, Satan will do all he can to block you in facilitating God's initiation. Anticipate some oppression and roadblocks. Ask God to help you see these for what they are, and ask Him to help you overcome these clever obstacles.

1. Developing listening skills. Sometimes people feel awkward when they ask an open-ended question and don't have a specific topic in mind. It feels hard to hear God in a "vacuum." If this was an issue for you, back up a little. Reconnect with God in a place that's familiar with you, perhaps through praise or through the Lord's Prayer.

Then, when you are connected and hearing Him, share your struggle: "God, I tried this, and I didn't hear anything." Or, "I tried this, and I really don't think I'm hearing you. I think if I write anything, it's just going to be me doing the talking. Will You talk to me about this?" Then let Him respond to you.

Trust that He wants to communicate with you, even if He doesn't wish to answer the specific question you are asking. Write down what He tells you and keep the dialogue going.

2. Blocked by not wanting to hear. One reason we may hesitate to ask God some of these questions is because we're not sure we want to hear His answers—particularly if we harbor misconceptions about God.

If this is an issue with you, please talk with God about it. Use one of the approaches below to start your conversation.

- "God, can I really trust You with these questions? I feel nervous about it."

- "Father, I'm not sure I want to open the door to talk with You about some of this stuff. Frankly, I think You're going to lower the boom on me, and I don't want that."

- "I know You're supposed to be My Father and Friend, but I've never had a conversation like this with my dad or any one of my friends. We just don't go here. Please give me courage to venture here with you.

- "Father, if we *do* talk about these things, what will You want from me?"

- "God, when I think of asking You these questions, I feel _____." (Use the feeling-words list in appendix C to fill in the blank.)

3. Hearing relationally. Remember that God's answers will be consistent with His character. Even when He is talking about a topic that might be difficult for you (such as correction or discipline), He will be loving, patient, kind, long-suffering, pure, compassionate, and joyful.

a. Look at your dialogue. What indicators of God's character do you see? (If you need a reminder of what God will be like when He talks with you, see the "you will feel" list under the "Pointers" section at the end of chapter 3.)

b. Did you allow space for Him to *relate* with you, or were you mainly concerned with getting information from Him?

c. If you need to, ask God a follow-up question that allows Him to relate with You more fully:

• "Father, I think I may have heard You correctly but missed Your feelings. Please share any feelings you want me to know."

• "Friend, what are Your emotions about me as You're saying this to me?"

• "I feel _____ when I hear You say that. Can You help me with those feelings?"

• "I'm hearing information from You, but I'm not sure I'm *getting* it. How can I go further and receive all You want to say to me?"

Remember to use all of the communicating-with-God skills we've covered so far. If you still find yourself blocked, ask God about it. Review the coaching in chapter 5, and work through with Him any portions that seem applicable.

Review: Communication and Relationship Skills

- Write down what you say and what God says so you have a record for later, and to help you focus and discern.
- Ask, seek, knock, and expect that God will respond.
- Talk with God as you would with a Perfect Father and Good Friend.
- Anticipate that He desires relational oneness with You, wants you to experience His presence, and wants to share Himself and His thoughts with you when you come and ask.
- Trust that He will help you discern because His Spirit is with you and is guiding you.
- Risk being vulnerably honest about your emotions.
- Expect and receive God's affection and affirmation.
- Gain God's perspective.
- Wrestle with Him.
- Receive His understanding and give Him yours.
- Enjoy Him.

RECEIVING GOD'S WISDOM AND DIRECTION

When most people contemplate actually communicating with God, gaining access to His direction ranks high on the list of reasons they want to acquire this skill. And yet, as you may have noticed, getting God's direction hasn't been an emphasis of this course.

I have been deliberate about this. In my experience, most of us naturally focus on wanting God to help us make the best decisions. If God would just tell us what direction to take in our careers, whom to marry, what to do with our kids, where to live, what ministry to focus on ... we'd be satisfied. We could move forward in life knowing we are going in the right direction.

Yes, gaining God's direction is wonderful and powerful, yet obtaining divine wisdom is not the greatest benefit of learning how to communicate with Him. Let me explain. If you asked my daughter or granddaughter why they love and appreciate me so much, it would grieve me if they said, "Because we have access to all kinds of wise direction through him!" I want their answers to be about who I am as

Dad or Grandpa. I am the one who loves them so much and whom they enjoy. I am the one who helps them feel loved and valued and cared for. I am the one who will be there for them no matter what. I want them to value relationship with me, not just value the wisdom and resources I may bring with me. The same is true of our Heavenly Father. He wants us to know Him and love Him for who He is, not just for what He offers us or the perks that come from having Him as our Father and Friend.

At the same time, it would be wrong to minimize the phenomenal benefit of gaining access to His ultimate wisdom and knowledge for our lives. I hear so many people say, "I wish I could figure out what the real problem is!" or, "I wish I knew what to do; there are so many options, and I can't figure out which one is best," or, "I don't even know where to start."

My perspective is that all of God's children have access to unlimited, exceptional wisdom for every part of life—both large decisions and daily needs. Our Father and Friend wants to direct our paths, shape the questions we ask, and walk us through everything we face. There really is no limit, no max, and no sense that we are using up this magnificent blessing. It never runs out and we never come close to overusing it. Isn't this incredible?

SEEK GOD'S WISDOM

A rich appreciation for God's wisdom is at the core of listening to Him for direction. God's wisdom tells us what is important to God and what His priorities are for us. His direction simply tells us *how* He wants us to implement His wisdom.

This is where we often get into trouble when we're seeking direction. Our pragmatic "Western" mindset focuses on action. When we seek God's direction, many of us expect marching orders somewhat like I received when I was in the Marine Corps. Then, I rarely lacked knowing exactly what I was supposed to do, when I was supposed to get up, where I was supposed to be, and what I should be doing while I was there. Often I wasn't sure how to do a task, and much of the time I didn't understand why I was doing whatever I was ordered to do. And for *sure* I did not feel particularly understood or cared for. But I did have *very* clear direction. That's often what we think we want when we listen to God: clear marching orders on what to do next.

Receiving God's direction is much different from this. He has far more for us than just giving us the bottom line. He is so relational, and His focus always seems to be the *process* rather than the end result. He likes to talk with us and listen to us. He is not about getting us to diligently do tasks and follow orders. He is parenting us and growing us and maturing us and enlightening us and enjoying us. There is so much that He desires to show us and reveal to us along the way *toward* providing the direction we're seeking.

Again, God taught me about this through my daughter. In her teenage years, she would regularly come to me with something she wanted to do and say something like, "Dad, I just need a yes or a no. I don't want lots of questions or instructions." Sometimes I would comply with her "nonrelational" teenage ways. But often I couldn't. I'd say, "Babe, we need to talk about this. Share with me what you're thinking; tell me why this is important to you." Sometimes I would say, "Why don't you tell me what you think I will say?" or, "What problems do you think I would have with this?" I wasn't willing to just say yes or even say no; I wanted to hear her heart and *parent* her. The same is true with God. So many times there isn't a yes or no answer to our questions. Instead we need to learn to relate to God in ways He desires and see our situations as He sees them.

So our starting place when faced with a need for direction is to seek God and His wisdom, His perspective, and His heart. When the Lord God was pleased with King Solomon, He chose to give Solomon whatever he asked for. Interestingly, Solomon asked for a "discerning heart" (1 Kings 3:9). The most literal translation for the Hebrew word translated "discerning" (or "understanding") is "listening or hearing." What Solomon actually asked for was a "listening heart" so he could make good decisions and discern justice for his people. Jehovah granted this request. This "listening, discerning heart" was what made Solomon the wisest king in history. And yet, the wisdom God presently makes available to each of His children matches the wisdom of Solomon. We all have complete and unhindered access to God and to His wisdom: "If any of you lacks wisdom, let him ask of God, who gives to all generously and without reproach, and it will be given to him" (James 1:5, NASB). I find this amazing!

LET GOD LEAD AND INITIATE

I cannot give you a "surefire" method for receiving direction because, as we have seen, God's ways and thoughts are not ours. In the previous chapters, we learned how to gain God's perspective and let Him lead our conversations. These are core skills to receiving His direction. The key is to let God direct the conversation so we do not limit Him to answering the questions we are asking in the way we expect.

At times, He will change our whole understanding of the situation. Our pressing need to resolve an issue can cause us to fixate on a particular question we want answered. But our perspective of the need may not even be valid. As we talk with God, relate with Him, hear His questions, and gain His perspective, our viewpoint changes and our pressing question is no longer applicable.

For example, I ask God for direction when I need to deal with a difficult person. Sometimes He responds by asking me how I feel about the situation. It's only when I start to talk about my feelings that I realize I am exasperated or disappointed. As we talk about this and as God shares His perspective with me, my view of the situation shifts. I realize the question isn't about how to deal with a difficult person, it's really about how *I* deal with disappointment. Suddenly, the direction I came seeking is no longer the point!

At other times, God may want to relate with us *rather* than provide direction. This is something that surprised me when I was first learning how to dialogue with God. I can remember asking Him which of three possibilities He wanted me to teach in an upcoming class. Much to my surprise, He asked me to weigh in: "Which one would you enjoy teaching? Which one interests you most?" I seriously doubted the accuracy of what I was hearing.

Then He said, "When Windy asked you, 'Dad would you rather me take gymnastics or piano lessons?' what did you tell her?"

I clearly remembered that conversation. I'd said to her almost the same thing God had just spoken to me: "Which one are you interested in doing?"

"Exactly," God told me. "That is the response from the heart of a good father."

Now most times God does give me specific direction and counsel. But sometimes He says, "I would like you to decide on this one. Whatever you decide will please me." I have enjoyed living in this freedom and joy with the Lord.

And often, God provides wisdom for my situation, but it isn't the direction I came looking for. In fact, it seems to me that His direction rarely is predictable. (Also I think He likes to expand my mind and enlarge my borders.)

I will never forget the time we lived in Virginia when, after a gut-wrenching season, I realized the job that necessitated our move there was abruptly and painfully over. The loss and how it had come about devastated me, Letty, and Windy. I needed to figure out what to do next and how to support my family. Through dialoguing with God, I pleaded with Him to give me clear direction. I wanted to know where He wanted me to look for a job and where to send my résumé and whether to change careers.

Much to my surprise, what He said was, "Take care of your family."

The next day I told Him I appreciated what He had said and I realized how important taking care of them was, especially since they were in such pain, but what I really needed to know was where He wanted me to look for a job and where to send my résumé and should I be considering a career change. He was gentle with me, and very compassionate and understanding. Yet after showing me great care, when He got around to the "direction" part I was dying to know, all He said was, "Take care of your family."

Since I am not the brightest of His kids, we actually went through a similar conversation one more time. When He finished sharing with me a third time, He gave me exactly the same direction: "Take care of your family." Somehow, after getting the same answer three times, I realized I needed to try to *get* what He was saying.

When I finally pursued Him and asked about the direction He'd been giving me, He asked me what would be the best way to take care of Letty and Windy. After thinking for a bit, I responded, "Well I guess we would go home to Texas, to family and friends—to those who care for us and would do anything for us."

"Exactly," the Lord responded.

I was excited and encouraged, knowing I was finally getting somewhere!

I was more than ready to take some kind of action, so I replied, "Okay, we are to move back to Fort Worth. Great, this is so helpful. So, Father, what do You want me to do in Fort Worth? Whom should I contact about a job? What career do You want me to pursue?"

What do you think God said? Yes, *"Take care of your family."* Then He explained. "My son, you are a hard worker and a great provider. I know you will tackle your next job with passion and focus. I do have work for you in Fort Worth. But the main job I have for you is to take care of your family: Help Letty and Windy heal from what has happened. This is your job; this is your focus. How I will provide for you and your family is more like an interesting side note. What you *must* be about this next season is *taking care of your family.* Do you understand?"

I was blown away. The transcendent, almighty God of the universe had given me direction with more clarity than any job or ministry "calling" I have ever had, before or after. I realized that apart from this very personal and customized instruction, I would certainly have missed God's direction. Now I let the Lord speak to me as He wishes and in ways that are way beyond me.

EXPECTING REDIRECTION

Along with expecting to receive direction from God, we can also expect God to redirect us. Redirection happens when God initiates with us and gives us a new direction to go in some area of life—often when we weren't looking for a change.

Sometimes God redirects us when we are headed into something that may be bad for us or others. We are taught in the Bible that the Lord is our shepherd. That must mean we are like sheep, which unfortunately often seems accurate. Sheep are not the brightest of animals; they tend to wander off. They easily get caught up in something or find themselves in dangerous situations; sheep are not to be trusted. A shepherd's staff is an essential tool, and one of its key uses is for redirecting a sheep headed in a direction that is guaranteed trouble. In a similar fashion, our Shepherd redirects us. He changes our direction and guides us so we do not harm ourselves or get into a dangerous or vulnerable situation.

At other times, God redirects us to align us with a plan He has in mind. We are taking care of business, following a path God put us on, when He tells us to stop doing something or to change direction— even when He had called us into those things in the first place.

At first, I struggled when I was redirected. I felt it was a form of correction or discipline; otherwise why would I need it? What the Lord has gently taught me is that He wants me to *follow Him*. He is not hoping I will finally figure out life so I don't need Him to lead me. He is the only one who knows everything, including the future and what lies beyond the next bend. His desire is not that I become omniscient and know all things. He just wants me to know and follow Him.

It is similar to when my young granddaughter and I are out on a hike. I know where we are going and how to get there. She does not. I want her to enjoy her time with me and be safe. When we are on a general trail but need to exit it so we can discover a unique rock formation and scenic overlook, she might say, "Grandpa, why are we leaving the trail? I want to keep going this way."

I have no problem with her question; I understand it. We are on a beautiful trail, one that I chose for us in the first place. But now I have something much better for her.

She may say, "I would rather stay on this trail." To which I explain that this trail will not take us where we really want to go. She may say, "Well, I would still rather go this way." Then I must be a bit more stern and remind her that I want her to have a wonderful time and that if she trusts me and allows me to lead us in this new direction, I am certain the reward of this "redirection" will be great.

The same is true of our Heavenly Father. He wants the very best for each of His children. Sometimes the way He leads makes a lot of sense. Sometimes, though, we cannot understand the way He is leading. The key is, who are we going to trust?

Recently I studied Acts 16:6-10, which describes the path Paul and his companions took during his second missionary journey:

Paul and his companions traveled throughout the region of Phrygia and Galatia, having been kept by the Holy Spirit from preaching the word in the province of Asia. When they came to the border of Mysia, they tried to enter Bithynia, but the Spirit of Jesus would not allow them to. So they passed by Mysia and went down to Troas. During the night Paul had a vision of a man of Macedonia standing and begging him, "Come over to Macedonia and help us." After Paul had seen the vision, we got ready at once to leave for Macedonia, concluding that God had called us to preach the gospel to them.

As I studied this passage in context, I saw that God had made His strategy clear to His missionaries. They were to preach the gospel in important cities, preferably in commercial and administrative centers from which the Word of God could then spread in every direction. Paul and Silas had followed this strategy and the Lord had richly blessed them.

Yet suddenly they are blocked from traveling into the province of Asia (modern-day Turkey). Most likely their plan was to go to Ephesus, a major trade and travel city. And eventually the Lord does end up doing remarkable things in this province, especially in Ephesus. So in no way does God block His word from traveling to Ephesus. Now is just not the right time. Rather, God redirects His missionaries.

So instead of going west, Paul, Silas, and Timothy determine to travel north. I suspect they thought, *Now this redirection makes great sense. In keeping with the Lord's church planting and strengthening strategy, we're to go north to the highly civilized province of Bithynia; we need to go to the important Greek cities that also have Jewish colonies.*

Yet they arrived at the border only to be blocked again by the Holy Spirit. Interestingly, we don't know how the Spirit did this—I suspect so we would not develop a theology of "how God blocks our paths." Now Paul and Silas and Timothy head in the only direction left; they go to Troas (imagine how frustrated they may have been at these seemingly fruitless miles of travel!). And it is at Troas that God creatively gives direction for the next leg of their journey. God's redirection results in the official opening of the gospel into Europe for the first time! Try to imagine how exciting and fulfilling this would be to the Lord's special missionaries.

As I allowed the Lord to open my eyes to this amazing strategy of His, I was quite impressed. The issue here was not Paul's mistakes, but rather God's tendency to initiate and redirect.

I've experienced His same initiation over the years as He redirects me. As a young man, my career in the insurance industry was going well. I tentatively accepted a promotion to Tyler, Texas, and tried to buy a house in the historic district. My wife wasn't settled on the house so I chose not to press the issue. Within a few days, an exceptional opportunity opened up in our hometown. God redirected me from what I wanted so I could have much more than I wanted.

We eventually ended up in Fort Worth, Texas, with me in my dream job. I made a lot of money; Letty and I were involved in significant ministry; life could not have been better. But God redirected me with a major career change. Tough stuff, but a much better fit with what God had been preparing me to do—and much more fulfilling.

I could go on and on. What I have learned is that I don't know what next year will be like. I expect to be doing the same thing I am doing now, which seems to be a perfect fit, just like the other situations have seemed like perfect fits. The only thing I know for sure is that I will keep coming to my Shepherd and I will keep listening to His voice and I will follow Him wherever He leads.

Sometimes God's redirection comes in the form of these major life changes, sometimes it comes through a much smaller change. Here is an excellent example of God directing and redirecting one of my friends when she talked with Him about her daughter's homework needs. My friend's creative, artistic, young daughter needed after-school tutoring—a consistently difficult task for her focused, intelligent mother.

Father, this afternoon, I must work with Sarah on her reading assessment. My pattern is to assume I can walk into this instruction arrogantly assuming I have what it takes to triumphantly conquer this tutoring—I'm smart, I've passed the first grade, I've printed up a worksheet. Sarah will most certainly respond cooperatively, compliantly, and logically to my instruction. Then I'm shocked and dismayed and frustrated and angry when everything goes wrong and I wonder how I got here again.

I'm coming to You, Father, and humbly asking for Your help and admitting and believing that I don't have what I need to tutor Sarah. I need You, Father. I want to have my soul delight in experiencing the richest of fare, the richest tutoring time I've ever had with Sarah instead of that usual failure I end up with.

Beth, you are listening to Me and responding and I am so pleased. And I find so much pleasure in giving You an abundance of rich help.

Thank You, Father. You telling me that I'm listening and that You are pleased makes me feel encouraged and valuable. Father, how can I begin again with a fresh start today, tutoring in Your power instead?

Focus on Sarah and your love for her—I'm more concerned with your relationship with Sarah than her grade on the assessment.

Will You give me the words and the touch? I don't have what it takes. I don't even want to be affectionate. "This is tutoring, not cuddle time"—that's the way I think. Will you take over completely?

Yes, Beth, I will. Thank you for being honest. Let Me surprise you and delight your soul. I want to share this rich time with you and for you not to waste your time on an unsatisfying afternoon.

Father, I am excited and encouraged. Your desire to do this for me is overwhelming. It makes me feel very loved and cared for. Thank You, Father.

The Father then went on to give my friend an unusual idea that totally changed how she approached the tutoring time. The next day, she talked with God about what had happened:

Father, thank You for Your rich tutoring time with Sarah yesterday afternoon. Thank You that You brought to mind using her little homemade art puzzle to start out our tutoring time. You reminded me of her little disappointed and hurt face when, tired of seeing it lay around, I had thrown the puzzle in the trash the night before. You touched my heart with compassion. And when I retrieved it from the trash, it was unbelievably clean and intact instead of gooped up. Thank You for preserving this little helping tool for me. I would never willingly have wanted to search through the trash. Thank You for showing me something to use that touched Sarah's heart—her art work. Thank You for giving me the ability to patiently let *her* control the rules of the game puzzle even though it made no logical sense. Thank You that this was a good first small step for me being able to show her affection and build a relationship with her instead of just enforcing rules all the time.

Thank You that she was then willing to work on her phonics assessment without the same defiance and frustration that she has shown in the past. For the first time, without me saying anything, I saw her try to grip her pen the proper way—this was Your doing, Father. And to blow me away ... she said thank you! Thank You for helping her do her homework!

Thank You, Father, for letting me hear those words from You through Sarah. That made me feel valued, Father.

Beth, I was smiling the whole time you and Sarah were together. I'm proud of you being willing to let go of your control and letting Me richly bless you with an idea that you wouldn't have thought of on your own. I preserved this puzzle that for days sat around the house for this very moment in time. I can take trash and redeem it for riches. I want to give you compassion and affection for Sarah. I want you to feel valued. I want you to feel My tremendous love for you.

I like to think of You smiling, Father. That makes me feel appreciated. Your being proud of me makes me feel valued and hopeful.

Are you showing me, Father, that art blesses Sarah's heart? That art is an avenue into a deeper relationship with Sarah? Our time together today using crayons to write spelling words went well, also. And for just a brief time, I realized how much I miss being able to create beauty in art. I like coloring with crayons. I liked it when I was a little girl, too. Sarah and I have that connection, that common bond of art. Are You touching on my longing to do this thing that You have created in me and weaving it into a means of connection between us?

Yes, Beth. You have seen this in Sarah before and I'm so pleased that you are now seeing it with My eyes. I'm sharing My beauty with you and Sarah, and I'm so pleased that you are enjoying it. I can make this gift to you both even richer than you can imagine and use it to bring intimacy into your relationship.

An intimate relationship with Sarah seems impossible, Father. Thank you for giving me a vision of what You can do.

I understand why it seems impossible. I'm glad you are being honest, Beth. I love you and Sarah so much and I've begun a good work in both of you and I won't quit on you. With Me nothing is impossible.

Thank you for accepting me even with my doubts. I feel accepted and befriended. With You, I have the best Companion to walk the road ahead and the power to not give up. "I am a friend of God."

Yes, Beth, I am your loyal "khesed" Friend.

Notice Beth's vulnerability in sharing feelings and voicing thoughts we rarely share with God. Notice God initiating with her in supernatural ways that show His Fatherly touch and practical, everyday guidance and wisdom. Beth receives and responds to how the Lord is directing her and how He is relating with her, and He takes things much deeper. Isn't it encouraging to see what the Lord has in store for each one of us when we come to Him desiring His leading?

DISCERNING DIRECTION

Many people are concerned with ensuring they have heard from God clearly when they are seeking direction. Truth is, the discernment process for hearing direction from God is little different from the discerning you have been doing throughout the course. However, I would like to offer you a caution.

A common conception people hold regarding receiving God's direction is that it will be accompanied by a sense of peace. Many people will not take action if they aren't experiencing the peace they expect. Now, while it is true that at times we have a nagging sense something isn't right and we need to talk more with God, it is not always accurate to say that "peace" is an indicator we are hearing God accurately.

Let me demonstrate. Suppose I hear a sound in my house at night and I'm convinced it's a burglar. God tells me to get up and investigate. Am I going to feel peace? Not on your life. Suppose He tells me to hide my head under the covers. Am I going to feel peace? No, I'm not. No matter what He tells me to do, I'm not going to feel peaceful about doing it.

Or suppose I am talking with someone whose goal in life is not to make a bad decision. She is extremely passive as a result. She has even broken two engagements because she never felt a peace about marrying. She has now received another proposal. No matter how accurately she is hearing God about accepting it, until she deals with her insecurities and fears there is no way she is going to feel the peace she is convinced she must feel.

Let's say I am counseling someone and God gives me direction that I am *sure* will go terribly; I have zero peace. I go ahead and follow God's direction. Sure enough, it goes terribly (this has happened to me more than once). But it has also happened that five, ten, twelve years later the person runs into me and says, "You know, I've been wanting to tell you how God used that awful time and used what you said, even though I was so mean to you at the time … "

A lack of peace will almost certainly be the case whenever God asks us to step outside the comfort zone of our circumstances or personalities. If God directs me to be vulnerable in a way that makes me feel not just humbled but perhaps humiliated, I will do it because I know God wants it. There is a certain kind of "settledness" in that, but I'm not going to be at peace. We have a choice to make when God gives us the kind of direction that has us saying, "I cannot do that," or, "I would fail," or, "I don't have the ability." We can trust God and feel quite uncomfortable and unsettled or we can trust ourselves and feel a sense of relief. Please don't let your comfort or discomfort be a major determinate in following the direction God is indicating.

If we choose to move out in faith, this doesn't mean we forge ahead with independence, maybe even swinging to the opposite end of the spectrum by saying, "Well, this seems absurd and I'm not at peace, so I must be hearing God accurately!" This is not a time for going at it alone. Allow others to help you, especially if you're facing a decision of significant importance. Tell trusted Christians what you are hearing from God and ask them to help you discern what God is saying to you and *how* He wants you to apply this wisdom and direction. Show them your written dialogue(s), explain a little of what you've been learning, and ask them to assist you in hearing God accurately. Often, others will see things in your dialogues that you are not able to see on your own.

DIRECTION FOR ALL OF LIFE

The more I teach others how to communicate with God the more I realize that what our Father wants for us is a *lifestyle* of relating with Him about everything we encounter. I want to be involved with my daughter and be there for her, not just dispense good information at key life junctures. I want to know about all that is going on in my daughter's life and be part of her everyday world. The same is true of our Father and Friend.

I am convinced that God's children can experience wisdom like Solomon's if they come to our Father every day saying, "Father, I do not have what I need for today, and I do not know what I need to know. But I do know You. Please speak to me. Grant me Your wisdom and understanding and discernment. And if I get lost or confused, Lord, I will simply return to You and Your presence." This is how I begin each day, and I can testify that God richly provides wisdom and knowledge and understanding and discernment that are infinitely beyond me (as anyone who knows how foolish I can be on my own would tell you!).

This habit of asking God for His wisdom and direction applies whether I'm considering what to teach in a class, wondering how to deal with an incident of mistreatment, planning a meeting agenda, or deciding what to do for vacation, how best to honor Letty on her birthday, or whether to replace a major appliance ... or anything else. Our Father loves to share His wisdom, His insight, and His direction for every day of our lives. Is this not a remarkable privilege?

May we trust God's plans for us, which involve Him revealing His sovereign will in ways we could never anticipate. Following His direction imparts life to us, allows His kingdom to rule and reign in our lives—and makes us excellent role models and mentors for others.

Practice Session

Skills You're Acquiring and Practicing

- Receiving God's direction by utilizing the skills you've been learning: dialoguing with Him, expecting His care and affection, sharing your emotions, receiving His perspective, letting Him initiate, giving and receiving understanding, wrestling with Him, and enjoying Him

Your Assignment

Do another dialogue with God, asking about an area of direction. You might talk about a major life juncture or you might choose a more daily need for direction (such as for a relationship need, ministry choice, meeting agenda, work project, parenting situation, or holiday plan).

As you talk with God, draw on all the skills you've been learning. Let Him initiate. Share your emotions and receive from Him. Wrestle with Him and enjoy your time with Him.

Pointers

- *Expect the unexpected.*

- *Relinquish control.* If you insist on having your exact question answered or expect God to answer it on your timetable, you may miss what He has for you. Come with an attitude that says,

"We're going to talk and I am not sure where it may go. That's okay, because I really do want to learn to trust You."

Follow-up Coaching

When you listen to God for direction, you are using all the skills you have been learning throughout this course. If you need to, see the review on hearing God (end of chapter 7) and on communication and relationship skills (end of chapter 9), and revisit any key chapter segments.

1. Key indicators. You are doing well if you ...

❑ Let God initiate and lead the conversation

❑ Gained God's perspective

❑ Related with God as His beloved child and friend

2. If you feel stuck. Sometimes we need an important direction question answered but simply aren't hearing anything from God. If this is an issue with you, give God a chance to initiate. Ask Him, "God, I've been focused on asking you _____. What other question(s) would you like me to ask?" (You may also find it helpful to review the portion on the silence of God in chapter 5.) Write down what God says.

3. Valuing information *and* relationship. Throughout this course, I have emphasized the need to let God relate with us. This is especially important when receiving direction, because this is a time when we often focus solely on getting information from God.

a. Look back at your dialogue, and mark any of the following that you felt:

Incredibly understood	Important	Supported
	Encouraged	Accepted
Loved	Comforted	Respected
Cared for	Affirmed	Secure
Valued	Appreciated	

b. If you didn't have much to mark, revisit the conversation with God. Tell Him that you think you may have missed Him relationally, and ask Him, "How would You like to relate with me in the midst of talking through this question?" (Be sure to receive what He tells you—see chapter 6 if you need a refresher.) Write down what He tells you and keep the conversation going.

4. Recognizing direction when you receive it. Sometimes God's direction comes "outside of" the question we are asking, such as when God told me, "Take care of your family." I heard Him, but I didn't get what He was saying.

a. Did God give you a direction that didn't fit what you were asking? If so, look back at your dialogue. Did you allow sufficient space to follow up on that direction so you really heard what He was telling you? Write down your assessment of how you did.

b. If you need to, revisit the conversation. "God, I think I heard You tell me _____, but I'm not sure I really get that. Can You help me?" Write down what He tells you and dialogue with Him about it.

5. Ask for help. Sometimes when I have a deadline on making a decision and don't feel I'm getting direction from the Lord, I ask Him,

"Father, do You want me to talk to anyone else and ask for discernment? Is there anyone You wish to use to assist me? Also, who should I ask to pray for me about this important decision?" If you continue to feel blocked in receiving direction, ask God these questions; write down what He tells you.

How to Verify You Are Hearing God Accurately

"How do I know I'm really hearing from God?" This is what everyone wants to know, and it is a healthy and wholesome desire. I am passionate that people feel secure and be able to hear from God clearly and accurately. What's encouraging is that God is more passionate about that than I am. He wants His kids to know Him and be able to communicate with Him. He desires to protect us from deception. I believe He actively does this and leaves His fingerprints on our conversations in ways that are clearly distinguishable.

In this chapter, I want to summarize these fingerprints into a list you can use to verify you are hearing God accurately. I have not found anyone capable of creating or generating these fingerprints using their own imaginations.

LOOKING FOR FINGERPRINTS

These fingerprints are measurable, objective indicators that help validate the accuracy of what God is saying to you. We have talked about many of them throughout the past chapters, but I want to pull them together in one place so you have a complete list. Following each fingerprint I will provide what to look for in your dialogues as well as causes for concern.

You will not need to go through this list after every dialogue, but as you are learning to talk with God, periodically check your dialogues with this list and ask God to help you. You won't find every fingerprint in each dialogue, but you should find many of them in your dialogues. If, as you use this checklist, you find that a certain fingerprint is consistently missing, pay more attention to that area as you talk with God—and ask Him for His perspective on it and what He desires for you.

Particularly if you have a dialogue that will affect your life or the lives of your loved ones in a major way, look for the fingerprints and ask God about the accuracy of what you were hearing. Ask Him if He'd be willing to condescend and give you a few more fingerprints. Also, ask a more mature believer who has skills in hearing God to read your dialogue, pray about it, and help you discern accurately.

If someone is questioning what you believe you're hearing from God, submit your dialogue and this list of fingerprints to a mature Christian who has solid skills in communicating with God. Ask that person to help you authenticate the accuracy of what you think you're hearing and what you're understanding.

The first fingerprint is one we've already talked about: ensuring that what we believe we have heard from God is consistent with His written Word.

Fingerprint 1: Scriptural Congruency

Above all, it is vital that what you hear from God is congruent with what He has already said in the Bible.

God is immutable. He cannot change. Therefore, He cannot reveal something to us that is inconsistent with His written Word. If there is an apparent inconsistency or contradiction between one of your conversations and the Bible, you are not accurately hearing or understanding what God is saying.

If you're unsure here, talk to someone more spiritually mature than you, someone who knows God and the Bible well. And, obviously, ask God about what you believe you're hearing.

In general, dialoguing with God should increase your intake of Scripture. If God is initiating with you, He will use His written Word a great deal. He will quote it, illuminate it, teach it, refer to it. One of the most impressive things to me is when baby Christians show me a dialogue that has a Bible passage paraphrased in it—and there's no way they could know the passage itself. Imagine how exciting it is to them when I show them the actual passage God was using with them!

> **Look for:** *An increased hunger for and delight in the Bible. Experiencing truths described in Scripture. Scripture increasingly comes alive as you read it. God brings up Scripture passages as you talk with Him.*

> **Causes for concern:** *Hearing anything that contracts the Bible. Conversations with God replace your time in Scripture. Scripture rarely comes to mind as you talk with God and God rarely directs you to His written Word. God seldom guides or comments on your Bible reading or study. Any pattern of dialogues that are "Scripture lite."*

Fingerprint 2: Parental Affection

One of the things that impresses me the most about our Father is His parental affection, which is a key fingerprint to look for in our dialogues. God's affection has dramatically changed me and how I talk about Him with others. Our God emphatically wants us to feel loved, understood, cared for, and very important. He is the ultimate comforter, encourager, and affirmer. Granted, He disciplines and corrects and rebukes and exhorts, but even then, He corrects us in such a loving, caring, affirming, motivating way. I really do believe that the best part of learning how to communicate with God and hear His words is His parental affection.

In the many years I have taught people how to communicate with God, I have read thousands of written dialogues. In so many of them, I am disturbed to see a lack of our Father's parental affection. Without this key indicator there is no way I can validate the accuracy of what a person believes God is communicating. It just does not have His fingerprints on it. Our God and Father *is* love; He cannot communicate in a way that is not loving.

Because this is who God is, parental affection and dedication and devotion will be observable if we are hearing Him accurately. Look for special names He calls you. I love it when He calls me "My son." Look for places where He speaks of His love and speaks to you affectionately.

Look for: Special names, increasing relationship, times when God touches you deeply by what He says, deliberate receiving on your part. Affection to the point that it may make you feel uncomfortable because you are unaccustomed to it. You will feel understood, cared for, loved, valued, important, encouraged, comforted, affirmed, appreciated, supported, accepted, respected, and secure.

Causes for concern: All information and no relationship. A God who only asks questions or interrogates you or instructs you. The absence of affectionate words and interchanges. No receiving on your part; when God says something affectionate, it doesn't "touch" you.

Fingerprint 3:
Correction and Discipline in a Loving, Creative Way

The next fingerprint to look for is receiving God's creative, loving correction and discipline. This fingerprint speaks of righteousness and love and grace. Because our Father loves us, He will regularly correct us and discipline us—but He will do so in a way that we still feel loved. I find this characteristic of our Father astounding and unparalleled.

There are two points here about discernment. The first is to look at the type of correction and discipline that are present. Correction and discipline that are not loving and creative do not bear God's fingerprints; He will not be harsh, condemning, abrupt, dismissive, or mocking.

The second point is that if your dialogues are "sin lite"—if they have little correction and discipline—then, based upon the Word of God, I would say you are missing significant key indicators. The Scripture says, "If we say that we have no sin, we are deceiving ourselves and the truth is not in us. . . . If we say that we have not sinned, we make Him a liar, and His word is not in us" (1 John 1:8,10, NASB). Scripture also says,

> My son, do not make light of the Lord's discipline, and do not lose heart when he rebukes you, because the Lord disciplines those he loves, and he punishes everyone he accepts as a son. Endure hardship as discipline; God is treating you as sons. For what son is not disciplined by his father? If you are not disciplined (and everyone undergoes discipline), then you are illegitimate children and not true sons.   (Hebrews 12:5-8)

The most distinguishing mark of being God's sons or daughters is that we are increasingly looking more and more like Him as He is shaping and changing us. I love what Jesus says to His disciples in Luke 6:40 (NASB), "Everyone, after he has been fully trained, will be like his teacher." We should hear others say of us, "You sure look like your Father." However, those who linger in shame and guilt also lack the marks of God's corrective and loving hand.

One of the most impressive indicators in this area is God revealing our personalized ways of quenching or grieving the Holy Spirit. If we ask the Lord to show us these patterns and then choose to receive His conviction and allow Him to change these patterns, God's finger-prints will be gloriously displayed upon us and in our conversations with Him.

> ***Look for:*** *Correction that brings you into a deeper relation-ship with God and brings a pathway for change; correction that causes you to feel free. Confession on your part that is received with mercy, grace, and joy. Freedom from sinful pat-terns and sins. An experience of "feeling" righteousness, when before the concept of righteousness may have been distant and intangible. Appropriate guilt as you acknowledge wrong.*

> ***Causes for concern:*** *Sin is rarely mentioned. Correction rarely comes up or is minimized. "Correction" that leaves you feeling isolated, sent away, condemned, "unfixable," dis-missed, or hopeless. Lingering guilt that leaves you feeling unclean, shameful, and unfixable.*

Fingerprint 4: God's Character and Mannerisms

Being able to identify God's unique characteristics and mannerisms is a distinguishing mark that assists us in validating the accuracy of what we are hearing. This indicator is somewhat more subtle.

Sometimes we have a good bit of God's content but we have inad-vertently filtered out His "feel." Consider the fruit of the Holy Spirit: "Love, joy, peace, patience, kindness, goodness, faithfulness, gentle-ness, self-control," (Galatians 5:22-23, NASB). If this is the fruit the

Holy Spirit produces in us, then these are the qualities we can expect to encounter when we communicate with Him. How could we imagine He will be harsh with us but produce gentleness in us? Or that He will be strident and impatient when talking with us but expect patience from us? Or that He will be unloving but call us to be loving?

Our Father can be powerful but He is gentle and tenderhearted. He can be fierce and bold and very direct but He also is loving and patient and kind. If what you believe God is saying to you is harsh or cutting or condemning or demeaning, you must ask for assistance or, at the least, validation from the Lord or from a trusted friend who hears God well. What I find helpful is to frequently refer to a list of God's names, characteristics, and attributes, so that I can know Him as He truly is (see the list in appendix A).

It will also help if you are aware of your "personalized" misconceptions of who God is. If you tend to view Him as harsh or distant, then you will tend to filter His communication through those misconceptions. Ask Him to reveal misconceptions you hold. Ask Him to help correct your view of Him so that it matches who Scripture reveals Him to be. This will allow Him to speak to you in His "real" character.

> **Look for:** *Words from God that bring life, that amaze you with how they carry both kindness and majesty, both power and gentleness. A tone that is touching, that draws you in, that attracts you like a magnet.*

> **Causes for concern:** *God sounds exactly like your misconception of Him. Harsh, critical, condemning, guilt-producing messages (these are often signs of enemy interference). A feel amazingly similar to your human parent with whom you've had a difficult relationship (this is very common). Or, God sounds like a doting grandparent to whom you can do nothing wrong and nothing is too good for you to have.*

Fingerprint 5: Depth of Understanding

Experiencing God's understanding is a very interesting "fingerprint" to me. Women love being understood; I believe God made them this way. Men, on the other hand, are fine with being understood, but it seems we don't care that much about it as long as we are treated decently. Therefore, a good question is, "Is a depth of understanding an important and valid indicator?"

Here is what I have discovered. "Understanding" is a foundational communication characteristic. Every man, woman, and child of every nation and background needs and wants to be understood. When we hear and receive God's understanding of our difficulties and trials and mistreatment and fears and insecurities, amazing things begin to happen. For certain, we feel much closer to our Father and more inclined to listen to what He has for us. Plus, we don't feel so isolated or hopeless or helpless. The best part is that our Father knows what we need to hear and what we need to do. All we have to do is listen, receive, and then follow. What a deal! I have found I love my Father's understanding; I have yet to find a male who, after truly hearing and receiving God's understanding, minimizes or discounts this wonderful fingerprint.

Look for this essential fingerprint in your dialogues. Our Father gives understanding in a masterful way.

> **Look for:** *Feeling words. God expressing His feelings about what you are sharing. Relational exchanges where God repeats what you have shared in a way that touches you deeply. A depth of understanding and attention that initially may make you feel somewhat uncomfortable. Understanding that compels you to go deeper, makes you feel safe, and helps you better understand yourself and what is happening.*

> **Causes for concern:** *No indicators that God cares about what you are experiencing. No awareness on your part of what*

God is feeling or how what you share affects Him. Little emotion. Factual problem-solving with no relational care. Rushing through difficult topics without giving God a chance to give you understanding (God cannot communicate with you when you are feeling burdened and troubled without giving you His understanding. Simply, this is not who our Father is).

Fingerprint 6: God's Lightness and Sense of Humor

We have talked about enjoying God and sharing His enjoyment. This is another fingerprint to look for in our conversations with Him. The Lord God is a perfect Father and He has an exceptional sense of humor. I love reading in the Bible about Balaam's talking donkey or the irony of God using a teenager with a slingshot to defeat one of the most imposing warriors of all time. And who can forget when Jesus told the fisherman Peter to go find the year's tax payment in the mouth of a fish?

My experience is that most Christians rarely hear or enjoy His humor. This is more of an advanced skill, and certainly the absence of His sense of humor in a dialogue is not an automatic concern. However as you become closer to the Lord and know Him in a fuller sense, you will appreciate and enjoy His humor as part of His affectionate relationship with you. I am impressed with how personal and "custom-fitted" His humor is for each one of His children.

At times when I want to make certain I have heard Him correctly, this has been a good indicator for me to see. I enjoy how He teases me and lightens things up when I have become too heavy. Our Lord is a Master at humor and He enjoys sharing Himself and many of His messages with humor. Please ask Him what He has for you with His humor.

Look for: Light relational moments that you enjoy with God. Appropriate lightness even in heavy times. Irony and affectionate teasing. Jokes customized to your sense of humor.

Causes for concern: Conversations that are always deeply serious, overly exalted, or hyper-spiritual. No fun. "Humor" that is taunting, harsh, mocking, degrading, or leaves you feeling misunderstood or put down.

Fingerprint 7: God's Perspective

God's surprising and "other-worldly" perspective is an undeniable fingerprint we should expect to see in our conversations with Him. I still find it amazing how rare is it that our perspectives match God's. When we are dialoguing with the Lord, He will intervene and correct our misconceptions and viewpoints. Our Father does not want any of His children to be deceived or mislead.

When we are passionate and unsettled, He will give us understanding, but He is also compelled to speak truth to us. In lengthy dialogues where we are pouring out our hearts to the Lord, it will be unusual that our perspectives will be accurate—and it would be unusual that we would end the conversation with the same perspective we had at the beginning. Therefore a common fingerprint will be the Lord giving us His unique perspective. Notice that His perspective will be true to Scripture, true to His character, and penetrating with its accuracy. Sometimes we will still struggle with this perspective and may not be happy with giving up our own, but most times we will end up feeling relieved, helped, encouraged, and "straightened out."

Look for: God's viewpoint is more impressive and customized than anything you could have come up with. You are left feeling invigorated and in awe of what's true. You feel lighter. Most times you will feel like something that was in dim, dark shadows now is being illuminated with stadium lights. There will be a sense of rightness, of righteousness.

Causes for concern: With frequency, you feel you can predict what God will say. God's perspective is expressed in generic, one-size-fits-all terms. You only ask for God's input on what to do; not His perspective. You believe your own perspective is accurate; you are invested in it and don't want to give it up (this is especially cause for concern in areas where you are in great pain).

Fingerprint 8: Direction and Redirection

Our Father and Counselor God desires to direct our paths, so another fingerprint we should look for is His direction and redirection. His heart is to instruct us, direct us, counsel us, and guide us into ways that bring life and light and success (as He defines it).

If we know how to communicate with God, we also have an awareness that we don't know the direction we need. We no longer tell Him, "Here's the question I need You to answer so I'll know what to do." We now acknowledge, "I don't know the right direction here, but You do. I am not sure I even know the right question to be asking." Once you learn this great truth, then you begin to understand practically what it means when Jesus says in John 15:5, "For apart from me, you can do nothing."

God's ways are not ours. One of the ways this will show is through God's redirection. A common fallacy is that if we accurately discern God's direction, then we just keep on with it. His role is that of a guide we are following who always goes before us. As any good guide does, He often redirects us to a new path because there's something He wants us to see or there's an obstacle He wants us to avoid. Our job is simply to follow Him as He leads out before us.

Look for: Direction in the context of relationship. God giving answers and direction that are outside the box of our questions. Direction that is encouraging and affirming, direction that is uncomfortable and unsettling (His ways are not ours). Daily direction because we don't have what we need when we wake up in the morning. Growing dependence on God. Increasingly giving up independence.

Causes for concern: *Lots of decisions and movement without God's input. Only going to God for decisions and ignoring the process or the relationship. You always are excited, comfortable with, and like the direction God gives you. Going in the direction He indicates but God isn't in front of you. Believe that God's direction always comes with peace (see Jonah and Job).*

Fingerprint 9: God's Initiation

I must add the blessing of experiencing God's initiation to our list of God's fingerprints. Obviously, when God initiates with us, sharing things with us that we never could have generated or taking us places we would never have gone or blessing us with something we could have never imagined, the Lord displays His "fingerprints" in masterful ways. It is unusual to have an extended dialogue with the Lord over matters of importance and not have Him initiate with us.

Since the Lord is our Master and our King, He will initiate. The absence of His initiation is a serious deficit as we look for fingerprints that assure accurate hearing.

Look for: *God introducing new topics, taking you in new directions, asking you to consider things you wouldn't have thought of. You asking questions that allow Him to bring up new topics. Pauses that allow Him to direct the conversation. Surprises from Him that may even touch your humor. When He initiates, He follows up and you expect Him to follow up.*

Causes for concern: You are entirely in control of the conversation. Only you bring up topics to talk about. Not pausing and giving Him a chance to initiate. You don't ask open-ended questions. Hesitation to ask certain questions because you don't want to hear God's answers. Not allowing God to follow up on the topics He initiates. God not breaking into dialogues when He wishes to interrupt and/or redirect.

COMMUNICATING FREELY, HEARING ACCURATELY

I have been married for more than forty years, and Letty and I have been actively practicing the relational skills in this book for many of those years. I truly *know* my wife and she truly *knows* me. Occasionally one of us has something on our minds we are uneasy sharing with the other. But even then, typically we pick up that "something is different" and ask about it. Very little gets ignored or pushed aside. And when we do talk, we are able to deeply understand and hear one another.

I have practiced the skills in this book with our Father for many years. It is very gratifying to realize that what I just shared about my relationship with Letty is also absolutely true about my relationship with God. I know Him and for sure He knows me. I literally feel *foolish* if I try to keep something from Him. And now that I am more open to Him and expect His initiation, if I try to ignore it, I guarantee He will not ignore it. He'll bring it up with me, just as Letty would.

In addition, just as it is very satisfying that I can now much more accurately understand what my wife is saying and not saying, it is very satisfying that I can now much more accurately discern and understand what God is saying and not saying. And when I am clearly off in what I believe I hear, He nudges me in very familiar ways and helps correct my understanding.

I want that same openness, freedom, and confidence for you in hearing from God. It's is vital that you are able to know each other and accurately communicate with and understand each other.

Fortunately we can listen to Him with confidence, knowing He wants us to know Him. He loves dealing with fears and insecurities and feelings of inadequacy. If we share any concerns or lack of confidence about communicating with Him, I am confident He will directly address them in a way that is customized for you and that uniquely addresses your concerns—because that is who He is.

Practice Session

Skills You're Acquiring and Practicing

- Using a list of fingerprints that let you discern whether you're hearing God accurately
- Allowing God to guide your discernment process

Your Assignment

Please do another dialogue.

If you'd like, talk to God about talking with Him. Bring Him any concerns you have about being led astray. Ask Him what areas of conversation He would like to emphasize with You. Ask Him about spiritual warfare and what to do with it.

Pointers

- *Relational conversation.* Again, remember to let God relate with you as your Father and Friend.

- *Facilitate initiation.* Allow space for God to ask you questions and initiate thoughts.

- *Stretch yourself.* Use the range of skills you've gained throughout this course. If you tend toward information over relationship, be sure to let God connect with You. If you relate well but hesitate to let God share information with you, pause and listen for this.

Follow-up Coaching

Congratulations! You're getting ready to "graduate" from the course. Now is the time when you are learning how to do the discerning on your dialogues and to let God coach you as you talk with Him.

1. Using the "Fingerprints." This time, practice discerning according to the fingerprints in this chapter. Before you begin, ask God to help you discern and to help you see what He sees in the conversation. Then read through your dialogue and the list. If you see good indicators of a fingerprint, mark that. If you see some of the causes for concern mentioned in the chapter, mark that. Ask God what He sees, and write that down as well.

> Fingerprint 1: Scriptural congruency
> Fingerprint 2: Parental affection
> Fingerprint 3: Correction and discipline in a loving,
> creative way
> Fingerprint 4: God's character and mannerisms
> Fingerprint 5: Depth of understanding
> Fingerprint 6: God's lightness and sense of humor
> Fingerprint 7: God's perspective
> Fingerprint 8: Direction and redirection
> Fingerprint 9: God's initiation

2. Trends in your dialogues. Often, you'll notice ongoing characteristics when you review several dialogues. For example

- You might notice that you pelt God with questions but never let Him follow up on His answers.

- You might see you do really well at wrestling but fail to lighten up and enjoy time with Him (or vice versa).

- You always talk about your concerns for others but fail to let your Father take care of you.

- You aren't addressing God as Father or letting Him parent you because you're still growing in how to trust Him as a father.

- You shut down conversations when God wants to get personal, because you're more comfortable with facts and information.

- You're eager to enjoy God and receive His affection, but you shy away from letting Him initiate correction.

- You really desire direction, but don't let Him broaden the conversation into other areas.

- You are discerning God's content well, but it's often missing His character and mannerisms.

It's okay to see these things! Growing in conversation with God is a process. As with any relationship, the more you experience Him as He truly is, the more you will trust Him with deeper areas of yourself. God is perfectly good and absolutely trustworthy. If you open yourself up to Him, He *will* take you to good places and will work *with* you. You will find He is investing in and leading the relationship with you.

a. Talk with God about what you think is going well with your dialogues, and ask Him for His perspective. Make notes of your conversation.

b. Now tell Him what you think are areas for growth, and ask Him for His perspective. Make notes of your conversation.

Results of Learning to Communicate with God

W hen I talk with people who have learned how to communicate *with* God, they all tell me it has changed their lives. They relate to God in an entirely new manner, and their expectations of prayer are transformed.

I'd like to share with you some of the typical results of learning to communicate with God in this relational way. Partly, I want you to recognize and appreciate what God has done and is doing in you. Praising and thanking the Lord is important—as well as plain fun! I also want to maximize the benefits for you. After considering some expected results, you can do a personal assessment to see if they match what you are experiencing. In any area where the described results are not yet personal for you, please talk it over with the Lord.

My goal in this course has not been to "change your life." I've simply wanted to assist you in connecting with the Lord so that God the Holy Spirit can do the exceptional work only He can do. He is the one who changes lives! When we talk with and experience Him, we receive the abundant life He desires for us.

ABUNDANT LIFE

The Lord Jesus Christ promised His followers not just life, but "abundant life" (John 10:10). Unfortunately *abundant life* remains a vague concept for most Christians. Learning how to communicate with God enables us to understand and tangibly experience much of what this abundant life is about.

A Sense of Security

Part of the abundant life Jesus offers us through learning how to communicate with Him is an incredible sense of security. Please try to imagine feeling unsafe, unprotected, exposed, or vulnerable when you are literally in the presence of the almighty, transcendent God of the universe. And I am not just talking about cognitively knowing you are with God; I am talking about relationally experiencing Him and His presence, the "You are with me" David affirms in Psalm 23.

So many Christians struggle with assurance. How can they *know* they are saved and are children of God and will live forever with Him? It's nearly impossible to doubt your eternal security with your Father when He regularly meets and speaks with you, reveals things impossible for you to discover on your own, parents you, touches you with His love and His words, and shows you how He is fulfilling His promises in your life. Actually I am going to go ahead and say it: I don't think it is possible to doubt your eternal security when you "come and talk with Him" in this way.

Peace That "Passes Understanding"

Then there is the peace "that passes understanding." In this world, who would not want peace, deep within our souls, that is beyond our ability to understand; a lack of worry and fear and anxiety? All of us know stories where people have a "peace" or "calmness" that enabled them to function at superior levels amidst the most adverse circumstances. I served in the United States Marine Corps during the time of the Vietnam War and have seen examples of this. For most of these people, these super-human displays are isolated events. Yet God makes a peace like this available each and every day of our lives.

We can have this kind of peace when disaster occurs, but also when something catches us off guard that would typically set us off. We can have this peace when a loved one is diagnosed with a deadly disease, and we can have this peace when a child is injured, and we can have this peace when we are told we are being laid off or when we are surprised by a major home-repair expense.

This peace is not something we talk ourselves into because our theology teaches us we're supposed to have it. This peace is a spoken peace, explained, and given by God Himself in a very personal, relational way. It comes only relationally with God, from living in His presence. And it is marvelous! Many would pay great amounts of money for such a rest.

Supernatural Power

There is also a supernatural power that is part of this abundant life. A power sustainable through extended periods, a power that is unlike anything we are capable of. "Super" power to raise children as a single mom, power to continue living when undergoing chemotherapy, power to prosper when experiencing injustice, power to withstand your parents' divorce, power to overcome horrible decisions from your past, power that works for every child of God in every situation we will ever find ourselves in.

When my dad was terminally ill, I agreed to lead his funeral. Yet when the time came I wondered how I could have been so foolish. I was in grief; I needed pastoring. How could I lead and comfort others when I was a mess? But there was no one else. My parents lived far out in the country and were not members of a local church (their pastor was Robert Schuller on television). I was in trouble. I had nothing to give and yet I knew I needed to be at my best as a pastor.

So I did what my Heavenly Father had taught me to do in times like these. I cried out to Him. I shared my feelings. I poured out my heart and my grief and my helplessness. I asked Him for His supernatural strength in the midst of my profound weakness. I asked Him to give me words of comfort and encouragement. I asked that all present would see and hear Him and not me.

Even though I really did expect Him to answer my prayers, it blew me away when He did. Dad was greatly honored; everyone was ministered to; everyone saw and was touched by my love for my dad and my love for my Heavenly Father. It was exactly how God wanted it to happen, and yet, in my own strength—no chance!

I have told you of the time a job was ripped out from under me and dislocated me and my wife and daughter. It devastated all of us. But the Lord was with us, not in some vague spiritual sense, but experientially, relationally with us. He met with us, talked with us, cared for us, accepted us, and helped us retain a sense of value through truth He shared with us, directing us and guiding us when we did not know what to do.

I have had many such phenomenal experiences of the Lord's power. I can tell you exactly what He said, what He was like, how He moved mountains for me, how He fought for me. You know what? This is what the Lord God desires for every child of His. He wants each of us to be able to tell engaging, suspenseful, entertaining, amazing stories—what God said to us when this happened and how He arranged things so that what could not possibly happen, *did* happen, and how He fought for us and encouraged us and supported us.

When Jesus promises us an "abundant life," He knows what He is talking about. This is what He is offering us if we learn how to communicate *with* God. But He has even more for us.

Actual Growth and Change

I want my life to count. I want to love sacrificially and I want to be loved unconditionally. I want to experience great joy and great fulfillment. I want to be who I truly am. Any good father would want all these things and more for his son. Our Heavenly Father not only wants all these things for me, He wants them for every one of His sons and daughters, and He is able to bring about this abundant fruit and growth in our lives.

Remember what I shared in the introduction of this book? The Lord gave me a simple answer when I was asking what brings transformation and growth in a Christian's life. He said it is entering into His presence. Anyone who truly comes into the presence of the Lord and is able to hear His words cannot remain the same. Everyone will be changed; we will be softened or we will be hardened.

To me this result of communicating with God is phenomenal! What else in all of life can make such a claim? If we learn how to come and talk with Him, we will be changed. We will become who we truly are and who we were made to be. And we will become more and more like our Lord; we will look more and more like Him. Others will notice and others will be attracted to these changes.

Deep Encouragement

Our Father also gives us deep encouragement as He lives with us. My experience is that those who learn how to communicate *with* and receive from God rarely stay in a discouraged state. It is difficult to stay disheartened when the Lord is loving on us and showing us exactly what we need to do to deal with oppressive feelings and situations. I am not saying you will leave God's presence singing and dancing, but it is very difficult to come to God, listen to whatever He wishes to say, receive what He says, and then leave in the same, discouraged condition.

The way our Lord does this is so amazing. Sometimes He encourages us by giving His perspective, sometimes by correcting inaccurate thoughts, sometimes by giving great love and care and understanding and support, sometimes by simply coming alongside us and bearing our burdens, sometimes by promising He will never leave us or forsake us, sometimes by reminding us of His promises, sometimes by providing a masterful solution to what seemed like an impossible dilemma.

Unusual Confidence in God

This experience of abundance leads us to an unusual confidence in God. For example, now when I experience great injustice or significant pain or a difficult loss, I am absolutely certain that after I gain God's perspective and hear what He has to say to me, my experience of what is going on will radically change. My circumstances may not shift, but I *will* experience abundant life in the middle of them. Common feelings of hopelessness and helplessness are just not sustainable. And fear—I have found fear very hard to maintain when the Lord is relationally and tangibly with me; I have never seen Him fazed by anything or lost or confused.

A wonderful example happened some years ago when our church, pastors, and elders were named in a lawsuit by a church member. The lady who brought the suit had left her husband to pursue another man. We had done all we could to call her back to her marriage, following Jesus' commands in Matthew 18:15-17, what is commonly called church discipline. All members were aware of this procedure, explained in detail in our constitution, and all members signed an agreement to abide by the constitution. Our attorneys asked for a dismissal on First Amendment grounds. At the district court we won a major victory.

Then the opposing attorney hired an appellate expert. The expert immediately saw the futility of the case and advised the attorney to change the lawsuit, making it a suit against only me, charging me for breach of confidentiality based upon the fact that I am a licensed professional counselor. Therefore, when the appeal was filed, I was now the only defendant.

Though we asked to have the case dismissed, the lady won the appeal against me. The court ruled that since this was now a simple case of claims by a counselee against a counselor there were no grounds for dismissal. The main problem was, the only evidence was about how the leadership administered church discipline—a clear First Amendment case.

We appealed this decision to the Texas Supreme Court. The case lasted five years and ended up costing more than a quarter million dollars. In the end, we won a unanimous decision at the Texas Supreme Court.

At first I was astounded that something like this was happening to me; I couldn't believe it. I was furious and discouraged and felt very helpless. I was accused of breach of confidentiality by national news sources and my local newspaper, even though the suit was based on allegations. Not only that, the allegations were false. Many, many people made judgments against me based upon allegations being reported as facts. And my attorneys drilled into me that I could not say one word to *anyone*. I was hurt, offended, upset, and confused.

So I came to the Lord and spent hours and hours over weeks and weeks dialoguing with Him. He affirmed me and comforted me. He empathized and shared in the injustice with me. He told me He was allowing this to happen. This was my turn to practice what I preach, He said, to apply what I had learned on dealing with mistreatment, injustice, and unfairness.

He urged me to allow His strength to be perfected in my weakness. He shared with me that if I chose to consider this trial a joy (James 1:2-4), He would purify and perfect my faith and trust. He said He would be my shield and defender, my advocate. He walked every step of the way with me and continually gave me what I needed for each day.

One morning well over a year into this mess, Letty spent an extended time dialoguing with the Lord. Afterward she told me that we should no longer pray for the lawsuit to be dismissed. I thought she was losing her mind, that the pressure and stress had finally caused her to snap. But then she shared what the Lord had told her.

God shared that Letty and I had been carefully selected. He said He had uniquely prepared us for such a trial. This suit would set legal precedence and would uphold the First Amendment right that you cannot sue a church or a pastor because you do not like how they do church. First Amendment rights had been eroding and our case was going to reestablish the separation of church and state.

God said He picked us for this lawsuit. Any suit like this had to originate with a small church that appeared to be helpless, because the goal was simply to set precedence and then go after big churches. In our suit, no restitution or financial settlement had been demanded. The desire was simply to set precedence.

God shared with us that most marriages and most churches could not stand against such persecution. But our marriage was strong and stable. Our church could withstand the onslaught. God revealed to Letty that our selection was a great honor.

This blew me away. My first reaction was that I never chose such an assignment; I never signed up. But after we talked and prayed and allowed God's words to us to settle, we agreed with the Lord. Our marriage would continue to grow and prosper. Our church could do the spiritual warfare that would be required. Yes, we would lose some members; that was a hard blow. But we had a core of solid believers who would stand with us.

As the Lord shared His perspective, which in *no way* initially matched ours, and as He led us and gave us words that touched our souls, as He supported us and gave us every day just what we needed, this five-year battle became an honor. We were able to serve and represent our God in a tangible way.

But many, many times both Letty and I agreed that without meeting with the Lord and listening carefully to His initiation, without hearing His perspective, without receiving His parental affection and affirmation, there is no way we could have survived such an ordeal, much less thrived.

The reason I have confidence in the Lord is because I have scores of experiences and times of conquests with Him. He is always with me and when I am with Him, nothing can prevail against me. Since He is always with me and I experience Him relationally, obviously I am never alone, and I am never hopeless or helpless. I know that nothing or no one can ever separate me from the Lord God and His presence, His love, His power, and His peace. How could life be more abundant than this, as long as we are here on this earth?

INTRINSIC LOVE

As we experience this deep, abundant relationship with God, we move from an extrinsically motivated love for Him to a love that is increasingly intrinsic. Extrinsic love is motivated by something outside of us. It is loving God because of what He does for us or offers us. Extrinsic love is good, appropriate, and valuable. When we learn to communicate *with* God instead of just *to* Him, we begin to love Him not only for what He can do for us but also because of who He is. This is an intrinsic love, a love coming from within. It's a love that … just is. It does not matter if loving brings no tangible benefit. This is the motivation David expresses in Psalm 42:1: "As the deer pants for streams of water, so my soul pants for you, O God." David felt a yearning for God just like the insatiable thirst of a deer—a thirst that cannot be denied and must be satiated. This is the desire of one who deeply loves God for who He is.

As we connect and communicate with the Lord, this inner desire will grow as a direct result. Instead of coming to Him because we need something or because we know we really should come or because we feel guilty if we don't, we come because we have to come; we must be with Him. Nothing else will satisfy. Nothing pleases God more than a child of His who is increasingly drawn to Him because of who He is.

LOVING ONENESS

Perhaps the most glorious result of communicating with God is truly connecting with the Lord God, knowing Him with an experiential, relational knowledge, such that true intimacy and *oneness* with Him is something we know; something we *taste* and experience.

I do not think it is possible for any of us to really grasp the depth of the unconditional love Jesus offers us. There are no conditions that will make Him love us more, and there is nothing we can do that can make Him love us less. As we learn to communicate *with* Him, we are able to feel and taste and experience and be enveloped in such a love. As the old hymn declares, "Amazing love! How can it be that thou my God shouldst die for me!"

At the start of the book, I shared with you how the Lord opened my eyes to Mathew 10:37 (NASB): "He who loves father or mother ... son or daughter more than Me is not worthy of Me." This posed a great dilemma, as I could not understand why God would make this impossible comparison the standard for being worthy of Him.

Now, after learning to communicate with Him, I understand. Now I do experience and have "oneness" with the Lord God; something that I cannot and have not experienced with anyone else, even those in my family whom I love with every fiber of who I am. What a wonderful result of learning how to relate deeply with our Heavenly Father!

AMAZING ADORATION

When we learn how to communicate with God, to enter into His presence, to hear and receive His creative parental affection; when we listen to Him share His heart with us, giving us His wisdom and insight—we are *compelled to* worship Him.

When the Lord is powerfully communicating with me, the only way you could stop me from worshiping would be to tie me up and duct tape my mouth shut. When I see the Lord as He really is, experience how much He loves me, and receive His exceptional parenting, it is similar to seeing the Grand Canyon for the first time on a beautiful sunshiny day. I can't help but praise and adore Him!

I want this same experience for you—for the rest of your life, as a direct result of having learned to communicate *with* your amazing Father and incredible Friend. He wants it too. Consider His promises:

Come, listen to me and your soul will delight in the richest of fare. Give ear, come to me, hear me, that your soul may live.
(From Isaiah 55:1-3)

I came that they might have life, and might have it abundantly.
(John 10:10, NASB)

I believe we can know what this means and actually experience this abundant, "richest of fare" life. May you discover it personally as you continue to communicate *with* your Father and Friend.

The Father's Heart

To all My beloved children who have been working through this book:

I am so happy you persevered, and I am so happy with you. I delight in You, just as I delight in all the people you have met in these pages.

I have so many things I wish to do with you and so many places I wish to take you. I have shown you only a glimpse so far; there is so much waiting if you will follow up on this invitation and keep coming to Me. Withstand your lifestyle, withstand your distractions, and keep coming to Me.

If you do not treat this as a course you have completed but as a relationship you have begun, doors will swing open to you that will astound you. All you have to do is come, and you will receive the richest of fare, direct from My hand. What you have read about in Scripture will come alive to you and be alive in you. This is what I have always had on offer for every one of My children. And yes, it is for you.

I am "hungry" for your life and hungry to live it with you. I am zealous for you. I want to inhabit your life with you. I want to go to work with you and have family dinners with you. I want to share all of life with you—your lonely places, your stressed-out places, your messes and your celebrations and your griefs. I want this. You cannot possibly want it more than I do.

I am the Communicator. I am the Word. And what's more, I am Love. Have you ever seen Love without an object? Without someone to love? Love must have relationship, and I'm offering it to you.

Take Me up on it. Try Me. Give Me space. Take Me in. Taste Me and see. You have now had a taste of Me; do not walk away; do not forget, do not leave the table. Stay here and talk with Me.

Practice Session

Skills You're Acquiring and Practicing

- Looking for fingerprints that let you discern whether you're hearing God accurately
- Letting God lead the conversation
- Celebrating with God some results of communicating with Him

Your Assignment

Do another dialogue with God. This time, review the results listed in this chapter and pursue one or two of them with God. You may wish to ask some questions and/or celebrate with Him over what He has done.

Follow-up Coaching

What a privilege is has been to introduce you to talking with God! I know our Father is pleased with the investment you have made.

1. God's fingerprints. As you learned how to do in the previous chapter, check your dialogue against the list of fingerprints and note the fingerprints that you see present.

2. Course review. Think back over your progress in hearing and relating with God since you began this course, and consider the following questions with God. Allow space for God to relate with you and give you His input.

a.   What do you think now is most likely to block you from communicating with God? Ask God, "Father and Friend, what is Your perspective on this?"

b.   How will you make communicating with God a life pattern, now that the course is finished? Ask God, "What would You like us to do, moving forward from here? What do You want for us?"

Final Words

Thank you for investing so much of yourself in learning this fundamental skill as a follower of Jesus Christ. If you have finished, I know you are experiencing great pleasure and delight and blessings from our Father.

Now, as the apostle Paul declared to the church at Thessalonica, "Excel still more" (1 Thessalonians 4:10, NASB). I promise you so much more is ahead. Our Father truly will honor His promise to give you the "richest of fare" (Isaiah 55:2). Continue to dialogue with Him and allow Him to continue to show you much more of Himself and of His wonderful plans for you. May He continue to bless you and keep you.

My heart has heard you say, "Come and talk with me."
And my heart responds, "LORD, I am coming." (Psalm 27:8, NLT)

APPENDIXES

ATTRIBUTES OF GOD

As you pray the Lord's Prayer, this list will help you "hallow," or "set apart," God's name.

Also use this list as you dialogue with God. For example, you might look at the list and consider what you need of God that day, and then ask Him, "God, I really need Your _____ in my life today," or, "I would like to feel Your _____ toward me," or, "Father, I need to taste and experience and have You shower me with Your _____ today."

Obviously this list is only a beginning; you can also use God's names (such as, Most High, Immanuel, Prince of Peace) and roles (such as, Defender, Counselor, Advocate, Healer).

Creative	Jealous	Righteous
Eternal/Infinite	Just	Self-existent
Faithful	Love	Self-sufficient
Foreknowing	Majestic	Sinless
Forgiving	Merciful	Sovereign
Good	Omnipotent	Supreme
Gracious	Omnipresent	Transcendent
Holy	Omniscient	Truth
Immutable	Patient	Wise
Incomparable	Perfect	
Incomprehensible	Providential	

Scriptures Related to Communicating with God

Read through these passages with the Lord, asking Him what He has for you in them and what He would like you to see about how He wishes to relate with you.

Even though I walk through the valley of the shadow of death, I fear no evil, for You are with me. (Psalm 23:4, NASB)

My heart has heard you say, "Come and talk with me." And my heart responds, "LORD, I am coming." (Psalm 27:8, NLT)

I will instruct you and teach you in the way which you should go; I will counsel you with My eye upon you. (Psalm 32:8, NASB)

For the LORD gives wisdom, and from his mouth come knowledge and understanding. (Proverbs 2:6)

Your ears will hear a word behind you, "This is the way, walk in it," whenever you turn to the right or to the left. (Isaiah 30:21, NASB)

Come, all you who are thirsty, come to the waters; and you who have no money, come, buy and eat! Come, buy wine and milk without money and without cost. Why spend money on what is not bread, and your labor on what does not satisfy? Listen, listen to me, and eat what is good, and your soul will delight in the richest of fare. Give ear and come to me; hear me, that your soul may live. I will make an everlasting covenant with you, my faithful love promised to David.   (Isaiah 55:1-3)

"For My thoughts are not your thoughts, nor are your ways My ways," declares the LORD. "For as the heavens are higher than the earth, so are My ways higher than your ways and My thoughts than your thoughts."   (Isaiah 55:8-9, NASB)

Call to me and I will answer you and tell you great and unsearchable things you do not know.   (Jeremiah 33:3)

My sheep listen to my voice; I know them, and they follow me.
(John 10:27)

But the Helper, the Holy Spirit, whom the Father will send in My name, He will teach you all things, and bring to your remembrance all that I said to you.   (John 14:26, NASB)

No longer do I call you slaves, for the slave does not know what his master is doing; but I have called you friends, for all things that I have heard from My Father I have made known to you.   (John 15:15, NASB)

But when He, the Spirit of truth, comes, He will guide you into all the truth; for He will not speak on His own initiative, but whatever He hears, He will speak; and He will disclose to you what is to come. He will glorify Me, for He will take of Mine and will disclose it to you. All things that the Father has are Mine; therefore I said that He takes of Mine and will disclose it to you.
(John 16:13-15, NASB)

The Spirit Himself testifies with our spirit that we are children of God.   (Romans 8:16, NASB)

That is what the Scriptures mean when they say, "No eye has seen, no ear has heard, and no mind has imagined what God has prepared for those who love him." But it was to us that God revealed these things by his Spirit. For his Spirit searches out everything and shows us God's deep secrets. No one can know a person's thoughts except that person's own spirit, and no one can know God's thoughts except God's own Spirit. And we have received God's Spirit (not the world's spirit), so we can know the wonderful things God has freely given us. (1 Corinthians 2:9-12, NLT)

If any of you lacks wisdom, he should ask God, who gives generously to all without finding fault, and it will be given to him. But when he asks, he must believe and not doubt. (James 1:5-6)

But you are not like that, for the Holy One has given you his Spirit and all of you know the truth. So I am writing to you not because you don't know the truth but because you know the difference between truth and lies. I am writing these things to warn you about those who want to lead you astray. But you have received the Holy Spirit and he lives within you so you don't need anyone to teach you what is true. For the Spirit teaches you everything you need to know, and what he teaches is true—it is not a lie. So just as he has taught you, remain in fellowship with Christ. (1 John 2:20-21, 26-28, NLT)

I correct and discipline everyone I love. So be diligent and turn from your indifference. "Look! I stand at the door and knock. If you hear my voice and open the door, I will come in, and we will share a meal together as friends." (Revelation 3:19-20, NLT)

FEELING WORDS

Many people find it helpful to have a copy of this list; you may visit www.ComeTalkwithMe.com to print one.

Misunderstood

Mistreated

Abandoned

Abused

Controlled

Neglected

Belittled

Put down

Ridiculed

Judged

Hurt

Disappointed

Offended

Alarmed

Apprehensive

Afraid

Fearful

Scared

Terrified

Anxious

Tense

Strained

Intense

Desperate

Upset

Distressed

Concerned

Nervous

Worried

Panicky

Sad

Unhappy

Despondent

Crushed

Dejected

Miserable

Oppressed

Heavy-hearted

Depressed

Despair

Regretful

Demoralized

Deflated

Defeated

Battered

Tired

Exhausted

Swamped

Overwhelmed

Envious

Jealous

Resentful

Prejudiced

Spiteful

Vindictive

Revengeful

Skeptical

Suspicious

Distrustful

Doubtful

Obstinate

Rebellious

Insensitive

Intolerant

Contempt

Critical

Disgust

Mean

Proud

Cranky

Impatient

Irritated

Restless

Agitated

Discontent

Reckless

Dissatisfied

Bored

Disturbed

Frustrated

Aggravated

Annoyed

Antagonistic

Mad

Angry

Furious

Lonely

Isolated

Left out

Lost

Ostracized

Overlooked

Ignored

Disconnected

Criticized

Rejected

Slighted

Alienated

Unimportant

Unloved

Small

Ashamed

Foolish

Disgraced

Degraded

Inferior

Insecure

Failure

Weak

Pathetic

Worthless

Hindered

Embarrassed

Humiliated

Dependent

Awkward

Clumsy

Uneasy

Uncomfortable

Unsure

Timid

Cowardly

Baffled

Confused

Perplexed

Puzzled

Callous

Numb

Paralyzed

Passive

Resigned

Powerless

Stranded

Trapped

Hopeless

Discouraged

Whipped

Broken

Helpless

Needy

Inadequate

Incompetent

Ineffective

Useless

Exposed

Shaken

Fragile

Vulnerable

Sensitive

Receptive

Relieved

Longing
Yearning
Wistful

Intimidated
Shy
Speechless
Dumbfounded
Astonished
Surprised
Wowed
Awed

Mellow
Moody
Reflective
Introspective

Calm
Patient
Peaceful
Relaxed

Adequate
Competent
Conscientious
Capable
Responsible

Independent
Self-confident
Strong
Powerful
Important
Sure
Confident
Brave
Determined

Optimistic
Eager
Energetic
Enthusiastic
Open
Interested

Tolerant
Caring
Concerned
Loving
Affectionate
Compassionate
Tender
Sympathetic
Understanding
Appreciative
Forgiving
Generous

Secure
Understood
Cherished
Comforted
Wanted
Desirable
Loved
Accepted
Affirmed
Appreciated
Encouraged
Contented
Satisfied

Excited
Cheerful
Silly
Amused
Glad
Happy
Pleased
Delighted
Joyful
Overjoyed
Thrilled

APPENDIX D

"VISUAL" ASPECTS OF COMMUNICATION WITH GOD

I wish to introduce you to "visual" aspects in your communicating with God. Our God is very creative, and He uses pictures and visual images to communicate many of His truths. Plus, many people are very visual and God enjoys communicating visually with those children He made this way.

The Lord God speaks of Himself as a shepherd, a strong tower, a hiding place, a shield, a fortress, a lamb, a king, the lion of Judah, a bright morning star, the light, the true vine, the bread of life, the gate, and more. These are visual concepts. My suggestion is to ask the Lord, "Do You have a way You would like me to visualize You, or a setting where You would like me to picture us meeting together?"

Some picture themselves walking with the Lord; sometimes His arm is around their shoulders. Some picture sitting together with the Lord in a special setting: sitting at His feet, sitting in His lap or being held by the Father.

You may also try using a picture from a Bible passage, such as the following ones.

Psalm 23. Imagine Jesus, your Shepherd, preparing a fine table for you while wolves snarl around the edges of the campsite, or resting with you beside a quiet stream, or walking with you through a dark, dangerous valley as you talk together.

Mark 10:13-16. Imagine yourself as a child with Jesus; picture Him welcoming you, taking you into His arms, and blessing you. Ask Him what He would want you to see and experience from such a picture.

Hebrews 4:14-16. Imagine entering heaven's throne room when you need mercy and help, and seeing the Lord Jesus Christ on the throne. What will Jesus look like? How will He call out for you? How will He welcome you? Imagine bringing someone with you knowing that Jesus always has time for you and anyone you want to bring along. Ask the Lord to help you see what He has for you in this picture.

Also look for specialized pictures He gives you. On an extended time with the Lord a while back, I was outside, and a bird landed on a vine close by and looked at me. I was amazed that the bird seemed to have no fear. He actually seemed to be enjoying himself and stayed on the vine just a few feet from me. I had a sense there was something about this scene that the Lord had for me. As I asked Him about it, He had much to show me.

By this time, I was delighting in having the bird there, and would have protected him from any harm or predators. This bird was completely safe with me and was the object of my affection and delight. The Lord said that was how He feels when I am willing to just be with Him, close to Him, in His presence. He told me how safe it is to be in His presence, even though most of His children never venture very close or stay with Him for long.

Now the image of a bird has special meaning for me, and God can use it to remind me of how He wants me to come and sit with Him. I am so grateful the Lord speaks so creatively in ways I thoroughly enjoy.

So ask Him about pictures and scenes, and look for His images as you read Scripture. If a picture comes to mind while you are praying, talk it over with Him: "Father, I'm 'seeing' a table in a fine restaurant, and I'm sitting at the table, but the other chair is empty. That's just the way I feel right now ... would You show me where You are in that picture?"

If you're concerned that your imagination is going to run wild and "lie" to you, talk about that with God: "God, You know how wary I am of imagining anything that isn't from You and claiming that it is. I don't want to do that. Is there anything about how You created Me here that You want us to enjoy together as we're talking?" Remember: God's Spirit is the *Holy* Spirit. Tell Him you trust Him to speak with you and communicate with you in holy ways and invite Him to cleanse your mind and imagination of anything that isn't holy.

Also talk with Him about dreams He gives you, especially if you are one who dreams often. Use the fingerprints list in chapter 11 to make certain He is the One who is leading in these visual means to communicate. Ask others gifted in this area to validate what you believe you are hearing.

APPENDIX E

STUDY ON MISTREATMENT, INJUSTICE, UNFAIRNESS (MIU)

First ask the Lord to show you what He has for you in this Bible study. Next, read through these verses carefully and meditatively. I find it helpful to copy the text of the verses onto one page, so I can read them all together.

1. Write out what you believe these verses are saying.

2. Then write out what these verses teach about MIU—mistreatment, injustice, and unfairness.

> 1 Peter 2:18-25; 2:11-12; 4:12-19
> Philippians 1:29
> James 1:3-5
> 2 Corinthians 12:9-10
> Romans 5:3-5
> Psalm 51:17

3. Next, write out:

a. How are we to view MIU?

b. What perspective are we to have?

c. From what you are learning in this book and from these verses, what does the Lord want you to do with MIU?

NOTES

1. Oswald Chambers, *My Utmost for His Highest*, January 12 (Grand Rapids, MI: Discovery House Publishers, 1935, 1963), p. 12.

2. A. W. Tozer, *The Pursuit of God* (Harrisburg, PA: Christian Publications, Inc., 1948), p. 9.

3. *My Utmost for His Highest*, March 30, p. 90.

4. Oswald Chambers, *My Utmost for His Highest: An Updated Edition in Today's Language*, December 13 (Grand Rapids, MI: Discovery House Publishers, 1992), p. 348.

AUTHOR

BUDDY WESTBROOK

Throughout a variety of ministry settings spanning more than thirty years, Buddy Westbrook has had one overriding goal: helping others learn how to skillfully communicate *with* God rather than just talking *to* God. As a licensed professional counselor and as a pastor, Buddy has utilized coaching-style leadership to guide many into practical, intimate, relational ways of connecting with their Heavenly Father. His education includes master's degrees from Dallas Theological Seminary and Georgia State University. Buddy is pastor of CrossLand Community Bible Church in Fort Worth, Texas. He and his wife, Letty, have been married for more than forty-two years. They have a daughter and son-in-law—both active in ministry—and a cherished granddaughter.

Printed in the United States
3123